The Charity First series aims to provide practical and straightforward guidance on the challenges confronting charity operations today, with fundraising in the spotlight. Its individual subjects range from those concentrating on the UK and Ireland to non-profit issues in the EU and other jurisdictions, from traditional to digital fundraising and from basic help for those just entering the third sector to specialist areas for the more experienced.

For further information and orders see www.charityfirstseries.org

BEYOND THE COLLECTION PLATE
Developing Church Income from Different Sources

Steve Pierce

First published in Great Britain 2015 by
Social Partnership Marketing LLP
38 Leconfield Road, London N5 2SN

Copyright © Diocese of Liverpool, 2015

A CIP catalogue record for this book is available from the British Library.

ISBN: 978-1-908595-33-1

Printed in Great Britain by CPI Group (UK) Ltd, Croydon, CR0 4YY.

Beyond the Collection Plate is also available in electronic format from www.charityfirstseries.org

CONTENTS

ACKNOWLEDGEMENTS

I am most grateful to all those who have helped in the preparation of this book. Too numerous to mention are the treasurers, finance committee members and clergy right across the Diocese of Liverpool who over the years have shaped my thinking and demonstrated faithful stewardship in their parishes.

My colleagues Kim Stanley, Gordon Fath and Cath Gaskell have offered unfailing support as well as giving of their time and wisdom in suggesting amendments and clarifications. Thanks are due to Mike Eastwood and to the senior staff in the Diocese of Liverpool for their patient encouragement.

Dr John Preston and Eleanor Gill have, as ever, offered excellent guidance and advice while colleagues in the stewardship network over 15 years have stimulated much thinking and much laughter. Rev Andrew Funnell and Mike Russell were kind enough to comment from a Baptist and Roman Catholic perspective respectively.

Robert Pike and Jim Myers of publishers Social Partnership Marketing have been patient above and beyond the call of duty in waiting for the final draft to land on their desk.

Finally credit and thanks are due to my colleagues at St James' House and especially to those in the Resources and Lifelong Learning teams with whom I work most closely. They never fail to inspire and make going to work a pleasure.

INTRODUCTION

'Here is Edward Bear, coming downstairs now, bump, bump, bump, on the back of his head, behind Christopher Robin. It is, as far as he knows, the only way of coming downstairs, but sometimes he feels that there really is another way, if only he could stop bumping for a moment and think of it.[1]'

Church treasurers and finance committee members may know the feeling. They are committed to the task but, bump, bump, bump, paying the bills, reconciling bank statements, committee meetings and the annual accounts don't give much space or time to work out other ways of doing it. Much of this work goes unnoticed and in some ways that is as it should be, although never taken for granted. For many there is the added worry of shrinking reserves and growing deficits. It can be hard. No wonder many churches like the treasurer to do the worrying and, let's be honest, some treasurers like it that way!

But our churches are facing a financial challenge which we cannot duck. Fifty years ago around three quarters of the cost of Anglican clergy was met by the Church Commissioners. Today that responsibility lies largely with the faithful folk in our pews. Anglicans, like myself, are where our free-church brothers and sisters have been for a long time: facing the challenge of paying for our clergy as well as maintaining our buildings and growing church life.[2]

This book is written for two audiences. The first is that faithful band of finance volunteers who do an incredible job of stewarding the finances of their local church. A little time reading and discussing these short chapters will open up ideas for increasing our income streams and a strategy to fund the fabric, ministry and mission of our church. In short, a less bumpy way down those financial stairs.

The second audience is that army of people who value their local church and want to support it. Many are in church on Sunday and their regular giving is essential to a sustainable church. There are thoughts here on key money tasks for churches and their leaders, different ways to give regularly, to give tax effectively where we can and suggestions for fundraising in a digital age.

Many more of this army of supporters attend worship less often,

---

[1] *Winnie-the-Pooh*, A. A Milne, Methuen & Co., 1926.
[2] See the handy leaflet from the diocese of Gloucester, *I want to know… why is the church no longer 'free'?* (www.gloucester.anglican.org/content/pages/documents/1354116327.pdf).

perhaps rarely, but they are delighted their church is there and they want to keep it that way. They may value the beauty of the church building, its pastoral ministry, those church activities or its community services, often in partnership with voluntary and statutory bodies.

Such supporters may establish or join a Friends group for their local church, make a gift to a fabric appeal or assist in fundraising activities. In addition, congregation and community alike can make what may well be their biggest, life affirming, gift to their church by leaving a legacy, a gift in their will.

The Bible tells us that a cord of three strands is not easily broken (Ecclesiastes 4:12)[3]. Churches need a funding strategy that makes the most of and blends together the several income streams available to them. Careful attention to this can transform the local church while a shortage of money can only constrain and diminish life, ministry and mission.

This is not a new challenge. Time was when pew rents and agricultural tithes helped fund our churches. Today church members are giving more than before and Gift Aid is a most welcome blessing. Fundraising will always be with us, bringing congregations and communities together and in a digital age can be more fruitful than ever before. But the hard truth is that we cannot hope to sustain our churches through funding events and appeals alone, no matter how creative. As every church knows the burden often falls on the same few people; they can be tired, busy or both.

Many of our churches are rich in beauty and heritage. All offer sacred space for congregation and community and each offers a witness to the life, death and resurrection of Jesus of Nazareth. If we value these things we must think afresh about the money that makes them possible. This book cannot cover everything but it will stir up fruitful discussion and suggest possibilities.

I am an Anglican and it shows. I have been a parish priest and a stewardship officer. I talk most about the Church of England because that is what I know best. But my Roman Catholic and Free Church colleagues tell me that principles in these short chapters apply to each Christian denomination although they will be adopted in different ways. Indeed it is important to note at the outset that generosity and almsgiving are an organic part of other faith confessions. For Jews *Tzedekah* is more than

---

[3] Biblical references in this book are taken from a number of versions of the Bible, including the New International Version (NIV) and the New Revised Standard Version (NRSV). For further information see www.biblegateway.com

voluntary giving, it is an act of justice and righteousness. In Islam *Zakat*, the obligatory alms tax to benefit the poor and the needy, is the third pillar of Islam while *Sadaqah* is an entirely voluntary act of giving at any time and at any amount. In Hinduism and Buddhism *Dana, giving*, is a virtue which may be expressed by giving to individuals or to public projects which relieve need.[4]

This is a largely practical book but as we set out it is worth remembering that we are painting a small part of a large canvas. In our consumer society money is more than a medium of exchange; it is an aspiration, a statement of worth and value and greed, personal and corporate, and drives much of the social injustice in our world. For Christians, how we think, feel and act around money is part of following Jesus.

As well as planting churches Saint Paul spent much of his apostolic ministry organising a financial gift for the impoverished church in Jerusalem. Never using the word 'money' he refers to his task as, 'the administration of grace' and calls those he sent to prepare the gift, 'the glory of Christ' (2 Corinthians 8:20-24).

How's that for a job description and person specification for a church treasurer or member of a finance committee! Think about your givers, fundraisers and financial officers in that same light.

When we manage money in the church we are managing the gift and the grace of God. So, with that encouragement - and that challenge - let's begin.

---

[4] Wikipedia offers an accessible introduction to these terms and the depth of thinking on this subject in each faith. See also *Altruism in World Religions* edited by Jacob Neusner and Bruce Chilton (Georgetown University Press, 2005)

1
MUST WE TALK MONEY?

The inter-war comedian Vivian Foster, 'the vicar of mirth', used to tell the following story. Two spiders meet in the nave of the church and one asks the other why he is on the move. He replies that he used to live in the pulpit but the new vicar preaches long and loud and he has not had a moment's peace for weeks. The other spider says, 'Come and live with us. We live in the collection box and we have not been disturbed for months!'[5]

It is a joke from a different age which still rings true today and reminds me of some words of Paul: 'Remember this: whoever sows sparingly will also reap sparingly, and whoever sows generously will also reap generously' (2 Corinthians 9:6). For 2,000 years Christians have faced the challenge of resourcing the life of their church, sometimes generously, sometimes sparingly.

That our churches need money is a fact of life. But, perhaps understandably, most of us don't like money talk, at least not about our own and not in church - and we really don't like it when the vicar does it. Not to worry; many clergy don't like money talk either and feel ill-equipped by their training to deal with church finances. Again understandably, they may hesitate to ask people to give more, not wanting to risk offence or to add a burden when people are hard pressed financially. Some are sensitive because the gifts of the people pay their salary while some, clergy and lay leaders, feel the church is about prayer and worship not bills and budgets.[6]

As every farmer knows, before seed is sown the ground must be tilled and prepared. So let's very briefly remind ourselves why money matters and how church leaders, lay and ordained, can prepare the ground for good money talk and practice in the church. It's a helpful exercise for all who have financial responsibility in the church while other church members and friends in the wider community may be a little surprised at what is involved.

Know your numbers

First, money is an operational necessity; we cannot live without it. Even

---

[5] In real life music-hall and radio comedian John Foster Hall (1867-1945), responsible, it seems, for the quote, 'We are here on earth to do good to others. What the others are here for, I do not know.'

[6] Clergy anxiety around money talk is well documented. See *'Clergy as Reluctant Stewards of Congregational Resources'* in Financing American Religion edited by Mark Chaves and Sharon Miller (AltaMira, 1999).

if our church became a museum today the bills for heating, lighting, insurance and repairs would still make a claim on our purses, wallets and bank accounts tomorrow and for a long time to come.

In the Diocese of Liverpool we have the world's first iron structured church building (and the second), the third highest church spire in the country, one of only three churches with a spire and a tower and a world class cathedral (two in fact; we've got one to spare). It's a reminder that church congregations of all denominations play a huge part in caring for the nation's heritage. But our churches are more than museums. They provide public space and continuity with the past. They provide sacred space for worship and celebration, remembering and grieving. The church may be home to a wide range of organisations. The money for all of this does not appear by magic.

So the first challenge to those responsible for the financial stewardship of the church is this: do we know our numbers? Do we know the trends in our income and expenditure? What about our reserves and our reserves policy? What is the giving profile and the age giving profile of our congregation? Like Fred the penguin in John Kotter's fable about change we may find that, 'the information was increasingly disturbing. The information was beginning to cry out: the iceberg is melting and might break apart soon!'[7]

I know some congregations are small, especially in rural communities, but wherever possible there should be a stewardship or finance group charged with exploring these questions. It cannot be left to the treasurer. As charity trustees we have a duty of care to manage financial matters well so we can achieve our aims. As God's stewards we have a duty of care to manage what God has entrusted to us.

Money and Ministry

Whether we are having a child, moving house, retiring, going on holiday or getting a pet one thing is certain: life costs money. It's no different for our church. When we turn out the lights after the last service then and only then will our church cost us nothing. Until then, as long as it has life, our church will make a claim on our purses, wallets and bank accounts.

More than monuments to the past our churches are maternity wards for new life and we talk money because it makes possible our ministry and mission. Church Urban Fund research suggests that churches in England

---

[7] John Kotter, *Our Iceberg is Melting* (Macmillan, 2006) page 9. For some financial analysis tools visit www.givingingrace.org/analysis

reach an astonishing ten million adults a year through community activities: food banks, healthy living courses, computer training, and lunch clubs to name but a few.[8] Again there are the costs of worship, administration and mission while churches with a paid minister or staff team bear the costs of salaries and perhaps housing. This may be a direct cost to the local congregation or met indirectly through a mutual system of parish share or common purse.

Sadly, for some churches the main financial task is cutting costs rather than growing ministry, which creates a downward spiral. Constant worry about money will diminish ministry, weary the spirits of both clergy and congregation and limit our vision for what our church could be.

So the second challenge to those responsible for the financial stewardship of the church is: *are we planning for ministry and mission by preparing and communicating a budget?* A budget is an essential tool but many churches don't have one and too many of those that do simply 'recreate yesterday'. They ask for a little more today to do the same as yesterday rather than offering a vision for tomorrow.

A good budget will capture, cost and commend the ministry of the church to the congregation. It will be realistic and robust about the present but should also enlarge our vision of the church's future. Keep the budget spreadsheet away from the congregation but share the headlines and connect your money and your mission. Don't list the youth club activities, talk about investing in young people as they grow in confidence and develop skills.

Money is a spiritual matter

The museum at Bentley Motors in Crewe holds a beautiful vintage Derby Bentley. The story I was told is that the owner returned the Bentley to the factory with a note saying that he had had the privilege of driving this beautiful car but it was now time for her to go home. Each year he sent the car a Christmas card and signed it, 'The Caretaker'.

What a lovely story and what a rich understanding of Christian stewardship: to hold something so lightly that we can both enjoy it and let it go. As someone said, perhaps Albert Schweitzer, if we cannot let go of something it is not our possession; it possesses us. No wonder the bible

---

[8] *Good Neighbours: How Churches Help Communities Flourish (2014)*. A 2010 survey by the National Churches Trust (NCT) p42 found that over half of churches host community activities. For a handy, practical guide to churches taking community action visit www.how2help.net

contains over 2,000 verses about wealth and possessions, way more than on prayer for example.

Those bible verses on money are pretty tough and most challenging of all they tell us that our money is not actually ours. Ultimately it all belongs to God and we are stewards, caretakers if you will, called to be faithful and accountable with all God entrusts to us (Luke 16:2; 1 Corinthians 4:2). The gift of wealth creates a moral obligation to use it well for ourselves and others. But money is also a temptation to self-assured arrogance (Deuteronomy 8:10-18). As I have written elsewhere, 'the desire for wealth is a heart problem and we are all at risk'.[9] The biblical prescription for a financially healthy heart includes contentment, humility, gratitude and generosity (1 Timothy 6:6,17-19).

So here's the third stewardship challenge to church leaders: *are we laying a spiritual foundation for living as faithful stewards?* As Pastor Andy Stanley memorably says, 'When it comes to stewardship and generosity, do your people know what you want for them regarding their finances, or do they just know what you want *from* them?'

Good stewardship preaching helps lay that foundation. Year round we should explore generosity and gratitude, borrowing and budgeting, saving and spending, lifestyle and legacy. Some churches offer courses which help people with financial capability or provide support, signposting or advice on personal debt.

Growing generous givers

As Christian Smith notes, 'a world without human generosity would be like an internal combustion engine without lubricating oil—pretty soon it would overheat and shut down'.[10] We need to talk money because generosity makes human beings flourish and is a core Christian value. Jesus said, 'where your treasure is, there your heart will be also' (Luke 12:34). What we do with money *reveals* our hearts; generosity *releases* our hearts from a creeping consumerism and helps us *remember* that God gives us everything.

So the final stewardship challenge is this: *are we helping our congregations to give generously?* Every three years it is good practice to run a 'stewardship programme' with biblical teaching on giving and the challenge to review and renew giving. Make sure that the traditional focus on 'time, talents and treasure' is not code for ducking the money challenge or making time and talents a proxy for our giving.

---

[9] *Your Money and Your Life* by Keith Tondeur and Steve Pierce (SPCK, 2010).
[10] *What makes us generous?* at www.generosityresearch.nd.edu/news. See also Smith's book in the Resources section of this chapter.

A simple annual review of giving is also good practice. Church costs rise each year just like our domestic costs. The annual review will address this but will also communicate the ministry objectives of the church, teach about giving and invite a review of how and how much we give. The annual review may be linked to communicating the annual budget, to a church anniversary, a patronal festival, a Gift Day or a special 'stewardship Sunday'.

Finally we should note here a simple but important annual task. Remember to say thank you to your regular planned givers in a letter and to the congregation in the notices, church magazine, website and anywhere else you can.[11]

Conclusion

Churches cannot and Christians should not avoid talking about money for money sustains ministry and is part of Christian discipleship. Generous giving is part of that prescription for a healthy heart and, just as with antibiotics, we must take the full course. How we can give generously and well is the subject of our next chapter.

Resources

Giving for Life (2009): an excellent and readable Church of England report which identifies four key stewardship tasks. www.parishresources.org.uk/givingforlife

Giving in Grace: a comprehensive stewardship website packed with thinking and resources. www.givingingrace.org

Church based debt advice and help for churches setting up debt centres is available from Christians Against Poverty (www.capuk.org) and Community Money Advice (www.communitymoneyadvice.com)

Jesus and Money by Ben Witherington III (SPCK, 2010)

The Paradox of Generosity: giving we receive, grasping we lose by Christian Smith and Hilary Davidson (OUP, 2014)

Preaching and Stewardship by Craig Satterlee (Alban Institute, 2011)

---

[11] For more on these tasks see the excellent report *Giving for Life* in the Resources section of this chapter.

2
MORE THAN SPARE CHANGE

The wonderful city of Liverpool produced Arthur Askey, Bessie Braddock, Ken Dodd and the Beatles and is home to a UNESCO World Heritage Site, the world's largest enclosed interconnected dock system, those famous ferries and, of course, Everton football club.

All this and so much more is due to the River Mersey which starts at the confluence of the Goyt and Tame near Stockport, perhaps a little higher at Compstall. Over some seventy miles other tributaries flow in but it is the Mersey which gives life and name to a conurbation of some 1.4 million people.

Other income streams which we explore in later chapters play their part but the direct giving of our congregations is our most important income stream and the one most closely linked to that core value of generosity. It determines much of the financial health and life of our church.

Practically speaking the numbers bear this out. For the Church of England in 2012 direct giving, that is planned giving (on which, see below) plus cash on the offertory plate and Gift Aid was a massive 63% of total congregational income.[12] My Baptist colleague assures me that free churches are just as dependent, indeed more so, on such direct giving. Spiritually speaking it should be like this. As King David said, 'I will not offer a sacrifice that costs me nothing' (2 Samuel 24:24).

Centuries ago the people of Israel offered their 'first fruits' to God (Deuteronomy 26:1-11). A basket of produce was fine then and still is in many parts of the world.[13] In an age of electronic money how might we offer our first fruits?

Loose cash gifts
Many years ago the Vicar of Mirth talked about loose cash on the offering plate in a monologue called 'The Parson and the Collection'. Many church members and occasional attenders still give this way, accounting for around 15% of the total direct giving in the Church of England. This familiar practice embodies a very important principle: a tangible connection between our economic life, our church life and our gratitude to God.

---

[12] This is unrestricted, recurring income which excludes one off donations and legacies for example. Tax efficient planned giving alone was just shy of £272 million which, with Gift Aid at £73 million, is half of this income.
[13] See the moving *A Handful of Rice* video at generositymovement.org/category/resources/videos/

Nevertheless, loose cash gifts are a vulnerable form of giving. Fifty years ago it made sense for most of us to offer our first fruits as cash or perhaps a cheque in the offering because this is how we were paid, how we managed our money and because we were in church to give on the plate at least once each Sunday. That is simply no longer true today. We cannot give cash if we are not there and that is not good for us or our church.

Now I know that cash still matters, not least for nearly one million UK adults who don't have a bank account. But today over 90% of us have a debit card, 28 million use internet banking and by 2018 perhaps just 2% of working people will be paid in cash.[14] But it's not simply a case of keeping up with change. How we give reflects the priority we attach to our giving. To pay my bills by direct debit but put loose cash in the offering may suggest that my giving is out of synch with my living.

In fact, *how* I give influences the *amount* that I give. You know the old joke: a £50 note tells how he often goes to fancy restaurants; a £5 note comments that he goes to church a great deal. Somehow in church £5 seems to be a lot of money! In fact we are more likely to use our plastic to pay in a restaurant and the truth is that how I give influences the amount that I give. The evidence is that cash giving is correlated with lower levels of giving. Half of UK charitable donations are made in cash, but these donations represent just 15% of total giving with the median cash gift (£5) being half that of a Direct Debit gift and a quarter of gifts by cheque or card.[15] As we shall soon see church giving is similar.

Partly this is because cash giving sets a low expectation threshold, partly because cash giving is vulnerable to attendance, circumstances and emotions. Each time we give we go through a mental 'donor process': do I want to give? Can I afford to give? Will it make a difference? How much should I give? Does this place deserve my gift? Cash giving means we go through this process *every* time we give.

Now cash giving is not going to stop tomorrow. For some cash is still king while others resist electronic giving and for still others the gift on the offering plate seems to go directly to the church and its priest or pastor. So some quick tips:

----

[14] www.paymentscouncil.org.uk. *On the Margins: Society's most vulnerable people and banking exclusion*; at the time of writing still available at www.consumerfutures.org.uk. Cash can help control spending and financial capability.

[15] UK Giving 2012 page 10 (CAF/NCVO). See the Resources section for details.

- The new Gift Aid Small Donations Scheme can benefit churches by up to £1,250. For more on this see Chapter 7.
- Ensure one off Gift Aid envelopes are readily available at all regular and occasional services and for tourists. A colleague mentioned that when visiting a church despite repeated requests no one could find him one.
- At such services, and where appropriate, courteously and confidently invite people to give as an act of thanksgiving. Don't be apologetic.
- Where appropriate, for example a wedding, make gift envelopes available to family members in advance of the event. A gift will only be an afterthought on the big day and psychologically people feel easier about a gift they *might* make soon, than they are about giving right now.
- Think about text giving. We are carrying less cash and more smartphones while electronic giving sets a higher level of gift expectation. We discuss digital giving in chapter 4.

Planned giving

Each week many church members plan their giving to their church using weekly giving envelopes, standing order or direct debit. A few will give though a dedicated charity giving account and a few via payroll giving. Each method of planned giving has advantages and each will appeal to different givers. What they have in common is that each is a 'commitment mechanism' that helps us to be *intentional* about our giving. We use our heads to help nurture generous hearts.

In planned giving we still ask those important 'donor process' questions - but not *every* time we give. We make and then commit to our decision so that generosity becomes a disciplined, joyful habit.

Why planned giving matters

We're all familiar with appeals from well-known charities to pledge £3 a month. These planned gifts are so important. They help charities plan their income and they help donors make a start and grow their giving over time. Churches depend on regular planned giving every bit as much. Planned giving has strong biblical roots, not least in the law of the tithe, a tenth of flocks and fields (Deuteronomy 14:22-29). St Paul gives practical advice about planned giving to the church in Corinth (1 Corinthians 16:2) and sent three brothers, *'to go in advance, to prepare in advance the gift you pledged in advance'! 'Then'*, says Paul – and this is the key – *'it will be ready as a generous gift, not as one grudgingly given'* (2 Corinthians 9:5).

This biblical principle of planned giving is the midwife of Christian generosity. We cannot honour what God has given to us and grow into generous givers if our giving is casual, careless or complaining. And this biblical principle cashes out.

Americans who planned a yearly percentage of income or a cash amount gave significantly more than those who decided weekly what to give. In the UK church three quarters of the top 20% of givers give via standing order; in the lowest 20% nearly half (44%) put cash on the offering plate.[16]

A move from loose plate to planned giving will increase giving to the church. People give more regularly and the decision to plan giving marks a subtle change in the relationship with the church and a step up a rung on the giving ladder. Giving expectations change and leaders can address planned givers in a different way in both thank you and 'ask' letters.

Methods of planned giving

Let's take a brief look now at the different types of planned giving. Each has both advantages and disadvantages so your local context matters.

Weekly giving envelopes

Weekly envelopes have been around for years. They are the most familiar method of planned giving and generate higher levels of giving than loose cash and cheques. Unthreatening, simple both to understand and use, envelopes are a good way for church members old and new to take their first steps in planned giving. They are also tangible. On the mantelpiece they remind us to give; in the offering bag they are a physical sign of our giving and in the prayer of the minister at the offering our giving is connected with our worship. Can I suggest three pieces of practical advice:

- Don't assume people know how to use envelopes, for example that they can bring two if they miss a week; so help them, possibly using some literature.

---

[16] Dean Hoge et al *'Money Matters: Personal giving in American churches'* (Westminster John Knox, 1996) page 76. *Giving Insight: a survey of Christian giving* (2011) pages 10-13; free download from www.parishresources.org.uk/giving. Average weekly gifts are: standing order (£16.46); envelope (£9.50); plate giving (£7.62). Note that averages are distorted upward by respondent self-selection and, for these figures, by the higher giving of the Salvation Army.

- Just taking envelopes won't increase levels of giving though it will increase regularity and therefore total gifts. There still needs to be an ask.
- Distribute the envelopes with sensitivity and a note of thanks. Don't just leave them at the back of church or hand them out as people leave.

There is, however a downside to envelopes. Like the collection tin, envelopes risk a small change, small giving mentality in a world of plastic cards and direct debits. They were designed for cash and cheques and are essentially a development of loose cash giving. More significantly as a giving mechanism the weekly envelope is not robust enough for the shifting patterns of church attendance and busy lives. People can find they are actually giving rather less than they think and I suspect that in too many cases envelopes are little more effective than cash on the offering plate.

As Joe Saxton, founder of research consultancy nfpSynergy comments, *'rather than have to ask people to give again and again we need to create mechanisms by which the default position … is to go on giving again and again without a further donor decision…. ways of giving that allow people to give and forget.'* Fortunately, such ways of giving are readily available to us.

Standing orders and direct debits

Nearly a third of people give to UK charities by direct debit, accounting for the largest proportion of total donations made to charity (29%; see footnote 15). For the local church, with some honourable exceptions, giving by standing order is the main form of electronic giving; on direct debits see below.

Standing orders and direct debits offer significant benefits to both the church and the giver and should be promoted vigorously where possible. The default position is indeed that the gift is made even when folks are not in church, thereby protecting church income from shifting patterns of attendance and our capacity to forget. Electronic giving eases cash flow, assists planning and administration and makes life easier and maybe safer when taking money to the bank. Finally as we have already seen giving by standing order or direct debit is associated with significantly higher levels of giving.

For the modern donor such electronic giving helps us practise that ancient and godly principle of giving our first fruits in the midst of the day to day pressures of a busy, consumer society. And, as noted above, how we give reveals the importance we attach to our giving, how much of a priority it is for us.

Standing orders and direct debits will make a big difference but it won't just happen unless we ask. Watch for the three P's. Don't *presume* that no one uses standing orders or direct debits in your church or that older people do not give in this way. Half of Matures give to charity using direct debit and a quarter make their first gift this way and are just as likely to do so as write a cheque.[17] Be *proactive* in asking people to give by standing order or direct debit and, as ever, make the ask as *personal* as possible.

The Parish Giving Scheme

The option to give to a local church by direct debit has been limited up until now, one honourable exception being the Gift Direct scheme in the Church in Wales.

In recent years the Anglican diocese of Gloucester has developed a successful Parish Giving Scheme (PGS). During 2014 the PGS moved into a national scheme, enabling the participation of all Church of England dioceses who wish to join. Over time this will enable the majority of Anglican church members to give to their local church by direct debit.

This new, national Parish Giving Scheme will offer all the advantages of giving by standing order plus additional benefits. All giving transactions will have all the protections of direct debit and once set up giving can be managed by a single phone call to a UK based team. A significant benefit of the PGS is that givers have the *option* to permit the Scheme to increase their giving automatically by inflation each year and a majority choose to do just that. Many givers do not routinely review their giving each year and so inflation erodes that giving over time.

There will be a phased roll out of the Parish Giving Scheme across the dioceses. When the time comes plan for a careful promotion and launch of the Parish Giving Scheme in your church. Experience suggests that the launch is most effective when combined with a giving initiative in the local church.[18]

It is well worth noting that dedicated charitable giving accounts, on which see below, are also based on direct debits and can be the platform for the planned giving of a local church.

---

[17] *The Next Generation of Giving in the UK 2013.* Access at www.blackbaud.co.uk

[18] Monitor www.parishgivingscheme.org.uk and www.parishresources.org.uk for progress and roll out of the national PGS.

Passing the plate?

People are sometimes put off electronic giving because there is nothing to put on the offering plate. This is understandable. We should not sever that intimate connection between giving and worship while giving nothing or making a token gift are not helpful, especially for newcomers, as we aim to create a culture of generous giving.

Fortunately there is a simple solution used by many churches: credit card sized 'giving cards' to be put in the plate at the offering. A giving card may have a picture of the church, perhaps a bible verse and words such as, 'my gift to God's work in this church is made by standing order'. In my own church giving cards are picked up at the back of church; in other churches a pack of 52 giving cards is given to the donor, just as with weekly envelopes. The PGS scheme furnishes givers with a plastic giving token which serves the same purpose.

Payroll Giving

Payroll giving is a government scheme which has facilitated £1.5 billion of income since launch in 1987. Employers must first register with a Payroll Giving Agency (PGA) approved by HMRC and the PGA makes a small administration charge. Employees can opt into the payroll giving scheme and give tax efficiently to charities of their choice through a pre-tax deduction from salary and, for those on pensions, through their pension provider. Payroll giving is tax efficient; it does not require a Gift Aid declaration and donors can give anonymously if they wish.

The advantages to both the church and to the donor are as with standing orders with the added benefit of reducing the administration of Gift Aid. In addition employers may make matching contributions, worth an additional £7.5 million to the £155 million given via payroll in 2013-14.[19]

Take up of payroll giving is low, however, with just 2 per cent of employers offering payroll giving and around 3 per cent of employees making regular donations. A 2013 government consultation aims to improve matters including a better web presence and a 35 day turnaround on donations.[20]

The way payroll giving works is a little counter-intuitive and it is most tax efficient for *higher rate tax payers* which can benefit either the

---

[19] Though payroll giving dropped by £21m in 2013/14. For statistics and guidance see www.payrollgivingcentre. com. Churches accepted as a charity for tax purposes by HMRC can receive payroll giving through a PGA.
[20] www.gov.uk/government/consultations/consultation-on-payroll-giving

donor or the church, whichever the donor chooses. An illustration will help.

Let's say that when donating under Gift Aid at the standard tax rate of tax (20%) I give my church £10 pw which Gift Aid increases to £12.50. Now payroll giving is *before* tax. If I tell my employer that I want to give £10 a week just £8 comes off my payslip plus the £2 tax on that £8 gift making a gift of £10. So I only give £8 and my church receives just £10, not the £12.50 it would receive under Gift Aid.

I must tell my employer to make a gift of £12.50 but only £10 will come out of my salary. That is why I say that payroll giving is a little counter intuitive. Have a conversation with potential or actual payroll givers to explain this.

Now, for higher rate tax payers the principle is the same but more money is at stake. At 40% tax a gift of £10 to the church will reduce take home pay by just £6. Alternatively, a payroll gift of £16.67 can be made to the church, an increase on the £12.50 at standard rate under Gift Aid, while reducing take home pay by only £10. The benefit is increased further if I pay additional rate tax of 45%.

For higher rate tax payers and for their churches payroll giving offers a certain advantage over making a Gift Aided gift being a single step process and arguably simpler to plan and understand. But the bottom line is that payroll giving requires a conversation with donors and some background information.

Charitable giving accounts

Dedicated charitable giving accounts effectively offer donors the advantages of a bank account, the protection of direct debit and the administrative services of a charity in making gifts and claiming and allocating Gift Aid. A giving account holder can make one off and regular gifts to churches, charities and eligible individuals, can distribute all their giving each month, choose to hold money in the account until a need arises or both. Gifts can be made anonymously and the accounts can be managed online, by post or over the phone here in the UK.

In the UK the largest provider of charitable giving accounts is the Charities Aid Foundation and within the Christian church is Stewardship. Both of these charities charge a small transaction fee which is recycled within the charitable sector.[21]

---

[21] www.cafonline.org; www.stewardship.org.uk

A charitable giving account helps us prioritise our giving through a mechanism which takes giving seriously and builds a sense of belonging to a community of generous givers while also offering all the benefits of electronic giving to the local church. Familiarise yourself with these accounts, include them as options in stewardship campaigns and annual reviews and make promotional information freely available.

Promoting planned giving

In one church the loose plate giving each week was at least equal to the envelope giving. Some years ago they had pushed standing orders but promoting planned giving had fallen away and in the absence of other options people put cash on the plate. This is not uncommon. A survey by Stewardship[22] found that half of respondents had been in church over five years before they started to give regularly. Christian Smith again: 'virtues like generosity….need to be actively prompted and tutored in order to become regular practices.'

Planned giving won't happen unless we ask. There is always a place for posters, notices and magazine articles but the key is *ask* people as personally as possible. Never leave individuals wondering what to do, having to make the first move or approaching someone they don't know.

Appoint an active *planned giving secretary*, although this title is a little misleading. There are administrative tasks but the secretary should also be accessible, proactive and able to respond to enquiries with knowledge and warmth in equal measure. It will always help to have simple literature about the different types of planned giving to help respond to enquiries.[23]

Weave the giving challenge and ways to give into induction sessions, welcome packs, discipleship groups, confirmation courses and pastoral conversations. Finally, embed the challenge to give well in your stewardship practice such as annual reviews, stewardship programmes or Gift Days. An annual thank you letter, untarnished by any appeal to give more, counts for much and helps individuals to realise the value of their planned giving commitment.

---

[22] *The Giving Trigger,* www.stewardship.org.uk

[23] For editable templates visit www.givingingrace.org/prepare-the-literature. Good practice commended to Anglican churches is to appoint a *Parish Giving Officer* (PGO) as a local giving champion. Visit www. parishresources.org.uk

That which costs me nothing?

There is a personal challenge in the words of King David with which we started this chapter which we cannot duck. We can each ask: *If my giving was returned to me each week or month, would it make any real difference to me?* If the answer is no, perhaps we need to think again about our giving.

Or, to ask a different question, *'what would my regular giving to my church buy if I spent it on myself?'* Again, if the answer is, 'not so much' perhaps we need to think again.

Conclusion

Practically speaking planned giving, done well and taught well, provides a robust income stream that has been shown to absorb the shocks of recession. Spiritually speaking each church member needs to grow in 'the grace of giving' (2 Corinthians 8:7). Planned giving is the trellis work that helps good giving grow.

Much therefore depends on the regular giving of our congregations. But churches also have friends in the wider community who are happy to give and happy to help. We turn now to ask how groups of these Friends can support the church they know and love.

Resources

Giving Insight: a report of a survey carried out across five denominations into giving habits and practices. (November 2011). A free download at www.parishresources.org.uk/giving

UK Giving 2012 (CAF/NCVO): an annual review of charitable giving in the UK and a mine of information. Note also the 2012/13 update. www.cafonline.org/publications/2012-publications/uk-giving-2012.aspx

Passing the Plate by Christian Smith, Michael Emerson and Patricia Snell (Oxford, 2008). An in depth review of Christian giving in the USA and interpretative comment with plenty of food for thought for UK church giving.

Stewardship charitable giving accounts: www.stewardship.org.uk

3
FINDING FRIENDS, MAKING FRIENDS

The beautiful church of St Alban's is home to a lively, welcoming congregation in the lovely village of Tattenhall in Cheshire. Their vision is to be 'a church without walls' and their Friends group is part of that vision. The Friends of St Alban's Church Building, Tattenhall is an independent charity with six trustees and some 130 members. The majority of members are from outside the congregation but are enthusiastically dedicated, as the name suggests, to helping maintain the fabric of their church.

The AGM in June 2013 celebrated £25,000 spent on church projects: a new boiler, flag pole and lighting and a Jubilee Path to the church door. Interestingly, not all of it is Friends money; they are good at match funding additional money from grant making trusts and statutory bodies so the Friends punch above their weight. Friends groups can have an impact on fundraising efforts.

Meanwhile the Friends of St Helen's, Sefton, one of 'England's Thousand Best Churches', celebrated their 21st anniversary in June 2014. Staying the course has built a Friends group some 380 strong, many times larger than the congregation and with friends scattered across the globe. The focus is the church fabric. Projects include a prayer desk to mark the Queen's Golden Jubilee, a hand carved oak bookcase to hold a rare, early 19th century history of the church and the restoration of two mediaeval windows. Less glamorous but no less important is the replacement of rainwater goods, routine maintenance and a contribution to insurance costs. The vicar, Nicola Milford says, 'it's quite simple; without the Friends we could not maintain this historic church.'

The Friends of St Alban's are among an estimated 900 church Friends groups registered as charities in the UK. The Friends of Sefton are one of hundreds of more informal Friends groups, just as effective as their charitable counterparts and serving as sub committees of the church trustees. Friends groups are growing slowly but steadily with registrations increasing by around 3% per year since 2006 and once established they seem to keep going.[24]

A 2011 survey by the National Churches Trust (NCT) suggests a lower figure of 700-800 groups. The survey finds that half of Friends

---

[24] The data is from Trevor Cooper, *How do we Keep our Parish Churches?* (The Ecclesiological Society, 2004; a free download at www.ecclsoc.org) page 52 and updated in a 2013 presentation.

groups are over ten years old and the rate of set up is increasing with a significant minority of respondents considering that a Friends group had real potential and 6% actively considering establishing one. Around two thirds of Friends groups are associated with Anglican churches and Friends groups are more common in rural communities (70%) than urban ones. The average Friends group will have 52 members with urban Friends, as we might imagine, having larger memberships.[25]

Money for God's sake

How can a Friends group help your church? Most obviously, and this is a primary purpose, Friends provide an additional income stream for the church. Just how much income varies considerably between Friends groups. Income of £1,000-£2,000 a year is not unusual while some Friends generate considerably more. A reasonable median figure is between £4,000 and £5,000 pa.[26] The NCT Survey suggests that Friends groups contribute an average of £2,250 a year to routine maintenance and nearly £4,000 for new or major works.[27] Note also that the income of a given Friends group can show year on year variations.

Three factors determine the income of Friends groups. The first is an annual subscription. Fees of £5-£10 are common with some rising to around £30 and joint, family and life membership options are common. While I understand the desire to keep subs low to ensure a broad appeal I do wonder if some Friends are selling themselves a little too cheaply. I suspect that a large part of the problem lies with upfront fees which at, say, £30 may make people think again. A monthly standing order at just £2 is worth £30 a year with Gift Aid and at £3 is worth £45. Standing orders also maximise retention rates, because there is no annual renewal, and reduce administration and costs.

The second financial aspect of Friends support is fundraising which in very active groups can dwarf subscription income. Some groups have a few headline fundraising events raising relatively large amounts while others focus on raising a little money from many smaller activities. The range of fundraising activities is astonishing: open gardens, village arts

---

[25] National Churches Trust Survey, March 2011, page 25-27. See the Resources section at the end of this chapter.

[26] A 2008 survey showed annual income ranging between £1,000 and £15,000 with a median of £5,000pa. (*Ten Friends Groups in Surrey*; Sue Filer. Ecclesiology Today 41, 2008). A 2014 diocesan survey in the south of England showed a range of £1,000 to £10,000 with a median of around £4,000.

[27] National Churches Trust Survey, March 2011, page 27. Actual figures are £2,278 and £3,783 respectively.

festivals, lectures, concerts and craft events sit happily with race and quiz nights, BBQs, raffles, meals and much more. Over time Friends groups seem to experiment and many settle on things that they do well, always with an eye to ensuring that the committee and its supporters do not get exhausted or have to expend energy constantly thinking up new activities.

Finally, as in Tattenhall, a Friends group income can be used creatively to leverage in funding from other sources: grant making trusts, statutory bodies and individual major donors, the latter needing a personal and direct approach. Potentially this is a significant additional income.

More than money

Back in the early 1920s, Chester, under the inspirational leadership of Dean Bennett, was the first cathedral to scrap the then customary six shilling charge for entrance.[28] Bennett wanted to make cathedrals accessible to everyone and his influence was persuasive. As a Dean of Salisbury Cathedral noted in 1925, 'it is far better to open a house of prayer to all comers … the atmosphere is quite different since we ceased to make a charge for seeing the cathedral: the voluntary offerings are double what we got by sixpences'.

Against this background Canterbury is credited with establishing the first cathedral Friends in 1927, modelled on Friends groups in support of the Fitzwilliam and Ashmolean museums and the Bodleian Library.[29] By the outbreak of WW2 there were 27 cathedral Friends groups. The cathedrals needed money but, as Judith Muskett notes, having become friendly they also needed Friends - and they found them. These friends came from near and far, from within the cathedral congregation and from among those who rarely, if ever, came to worship but valued all that cathedrals offer.

Local churches, it seems, took their cue from the cathedrals and the same principles apply. Many in our communities do not attend worship but love - and the word is not too strong[30] - their church. They value its heritage, sacred space, its place in their community and personal memory.

[28] I have drawn here on the work of Judith Muskett, *From Sixpenny Entry to Five Shilling Subscription: Charting Cathedral Outreach and Friends' Associations in the 1920s and 1930s* (Journal of Anglican Studies Vol 10 pages 94-118).

[29] Another cathedral makes a claim to hosting the first Friends group: Liverpool of course! In May 1925 Sir Frederick Radcliffe established 'The Builders', to make it possible for ordinary people to contribute to the building of Liverpool Cathedral, the first part of which had been consecrated in 1924.

[30] Judith Muskett strongly argues that the word 'Friend' is entirely appropriate when used of the relationship between people and a building. *'Friends' of Anglican cathedrals: norms and values. Befriending, friending or misnomer?* (Journal of Beliefs & Values: Studies in Religion & Education, 34:2, pages 189-203).

As the chair of a Friends group said to me, 'if it was not for a recent legacy we would be completely lost without our Friends'.

A Friends group, therefore, offers people a way to support their church without *necessarily* being regular worshippers and thousands of men and women do just that. A little under half of Friends are not members of their local congregation with perhaps 22,000 non congregational members across the country supporting their local church.[31] My own conversations with Friends groups lead me to the same conclusion.

Friends groups bring in welcome additional money but the name 'Friends' is no accident. Friends groups help build what the sociologists call 'social capital' and the rest of us know as good, healthy relationships and the things that get done together. So back at St Alban's the energetic Rector, Father Lameck Mutete, says, 'The Friends group is one of the ways we can take the church back to the community; it is after all a parish church. Even if they don't attend people here love their church but often they don't know how to help us. The Friends group is one of the ways they can help'.

The declared purpose of one Friends group is, 'to preserve our ancient and historic church for the use of future generations and to give pleasure to our community'. The most successful Friends groups I have spoken to have fundraising activities which have become part of the social fabric of their community. They raise money and they build that social capital. As Trevor Cooper notes, some Friends groups 'are clearly a force for social cohesion in their own right'.[32]

Just for the building?

Understandably most church Friends groups attend to the fabric needs of the church. They focus on the maintenance and often the beautification of the church and how our churches need that support. The joy of these well-loved buildings is matched only by the challenge of maintaining them, especially where congregations are small. But a Friends group does not *always* need to be calibrated around the church building.

Churches of all denominations leave their imprint on those whose lives they touch. It may be Sunday School, the uniformed organisations,

---

[31] NCT Survey 2011 page 26.
[32] *How do we keep our parish churches?* page 53. 'A challenge for cathedral Friends' associations is to preserve for future generations not only cathedral fabric but also key norms and values of friendship, against the prevailing trends of an apparently increasingly individuated culture' Muskett, *'Friends' of Anglican Cathedrals* page 201.

the influence of a prayerful priest or the pastoral support of a loving congregation. A church may have nurtured gifts, fostered vocation or profoundly marked the passage of life and death for individuals or families. It will have formed the spiritual life of many over generations and may have gifted clergy, youth leaders, Sunday school teachers and faithful congregation members to the wider church. People who have been formed by a church's ministry are potential Friends and many will, if asked, give financially to support a church's life and ministry.

Making friends

First things first. The centre of gravity of a Friends group must lie in the community and not in the church congregation. Every conversation I have ever had with the chair of a successful Friends groups stresses this point.

Now, back in Tattenhall the Chair of the Friends, Bob Blackhurst, is indeed a member of the congregation but the independent Friends group is the focus of his ministry and this is not unusual. Of course, congregation members can and do become Friends and may serve on the committee. In fact if the average membership of a Friends group is 52 then 28 of them will also be in the congregation on Sunday. But it is the wider community, not the congregation, that determines the DNA of a Friends group. You will need a strong chair and a committee that represents the wider community.

It is also worth clarifying that Friends offer *financial* support for their church. Of course, *some* Friends will also give their time and offer their talents, making tea or levelling flagstones and this is always welcome. But be clear that this is an additional voluntary role and neither required or expected of Friends. Indeed, most Friends will not be volunteers.[33]

So before going public with press and posters or tweeting and trending on Twitter consider the five Ps of a well-run Friends group: purpose, proposition, promotion, patron, and payback.

Purpose

Be absolutely clear about the purpose of your proposed Friends group. Define the objectives and write them down. If the Friends is to be a separate charity (on which, see below) this will be in the constitution.[34]

---

[33] If we want a Friends group which will give time and talents primarily then be clear about this. www. churchcare.co.uk lists three types of Friends (under the Open and Sustainable menu) which they refer to as passive supporters, active friends and dedicated trusts. Be clear what you want.

[34] See the Resources section for model constitutions. For useful tips on constitutions see the Friends section of the Churches Trust for Cumbria website (www.ctfc.org.uk).

Otherwise capture your purpose in the committee terms of reference or trustee minutes. Are you about maintenance, beautification or both? Do the Friends help look after the graveyard? Will they, like Sefton Friends, help with insurance costs or maybe security measures? Is it clearly stated that the church is a living place of worship? You will reflect this purpose in promotional literature produced by the Friends.

Linked to purpose, who will become your Friends? In many cases most Friends are found within the local community. But where there is a beautiful building of architectural merit or with an eclectic musical or worship tradition or perhaps a focus on former members supporting ministry then Friends may be drawn from a much wider area. The question is always, what do people want to give to, what moves them, what do they want to support?

This is also the place to clarify the relationship between the Friends group and the church council or trustees who have legal responsibility for the building. The Tattenhall annual report notes in passing that, 'all projects have to be agreed with the PCC; this procedure works well'. A lot of personal trust and conversations underwrite that simple statement so build this trust early doors.

I know of two church councils that want to install toilets in the church and two Friends groups that don't feel that this is something they can support. In both cases good relationships and clarity of purpose make for understanding and lack of tension - but it could be very different. A clear purpose goes a long way to ensuring those good relationships. So talk; agree on the needs of the church and how the Friends can help and be clear about the respective responsibilities and activities of both trustees and Friends.

Proposition

Be clear about what you are asking Friends to do. First, establish what subscription level is appropriate for your particular Friends group. As a rule of thumb the more active the group's fundraising efforts the lower the subs can be. This is also the place to consider the activities of the Friends group. Fundraising is an obvious activity and it will help to outline what kind of commitment is involved. Friends groups may also offer annual lectures or cultural events. Be clear about what you want to achieve and also who you need to talk with locally if you are to succeed.

Promotion

You will need to promote your new group. The discipline of preparing a traditional leaflet can help you capture your core purpose in words. Posters in libraries, hand delivered brochures, adverts in shops, church magazines and local newspapers and air time on local radio are common ways to promote a group. In a lonely and beautiful church in Herefordshire I picked up a nicely produced postcard advertising the Friends group. Some groups produce excellent websites[35] or pages within the church website. Get social media working for you at a launch event which might be at a patronal festival or special church anniversary and post photographs afterwards. Beyond your immediate community you may decide to list potential supporters: former church members, tourists, baptism and wedding contacts. There are many possibilities, the choice is yours.

Patron

Professor Plum or Lady Penelope can serve as a patron and advocate of the Friends as can a well-known local historian, radio presenter or a former Rector. It's not just the name; it is the personal invitation to join the Friends, a face on the literature, a voice at the launch event.

But 'patron' here is also code for a committed chair and committee, people who will shape and lead the work of the Friends. Every conversation I have affirms the importance of a good chair and committee who will, as above, keep the centre of gravity in the community. The Friends cannot be an additional responsibility for the church council to shoulder.

Payback

Friends have benefits; in the arts and cultural sectors benefits may include ticket discounts or the members bar! In a church context benefits should not be excessive but they should be thought about and appropriate to your context. A special carol service invite, an annual lecture or a meal are possibilities while an annual thank you letter is always appreciated. Note that some benefits can compromise Gift Aid so seek advice if you are not sure.

Decide also how and how often you will communicate to your Friends. A hard copy newsletter is popular but factor in the costs of printing and postage. Email can work well when done well and always do what you can, not what you cannot, when it comes to websites and social media.

---

[35] See, for example, www.friendsofbordenchurch.co.uk

Finally, Friends value achieving specific, tangible and visible projects. It may be a refurbished organ or a repaired clock but try to plan in some quick wins at the outset and achievable objectives each year.

Practicalities

The Resource section of this chapter points to excellent practical guidance on structure. Briefly, therefore, there are two main options worth knowing at the outset but decide which works for you in the light of your conversations. Like Tattenhall, many Friends groups are separate charities with their own trustees and make grants to the church according to their constitution. This structure is often chosen deliberately to stress that the Friends are distinct from the congregation and to make a Friends group attractive to non-worshippers. Potentially this may also give access to funds that the church body may not be able to obtain.

The downside is that a separate charity requires governance and in a worst case scenario a group with a vested interest in the building can institutionalise disagreement or conflict with the church trustees although this is rare.

The second option, adopted by the Sefton Friends, is to structure the Friends as a sub-committee of the church council/trustees. All Friends money is held in a restricted fund in the church accounts to be used for the stated purposes of the Friends group. The upside is that those who have a duty of care also have access to the funds that help them to discharge that duty. The downside is that the Friends *may* be perceived as too close to the church community by those outside of the immediate congregation. However, careful writing of the terms of reference is usually sufficient to put an appropriate distance between the Friends and the worshipping congregation.

Conclusion

A Friends group offers a potentially significant additional income stream which is usually but not always focused on the maintenance and beautification of the fabric of the church. The key ingredients for success are a strong chair and active committee, a good relationship with the church council, a centre of gravity in the wider community and some visible, tangible things that Friends can achieve and celebrate.

Resources

A Friends' Scheme for a Parish Church. This classic booklet from the Diocese of Canterbury is full of practical tips and advice. Download at www.parishresources.org.uk/friends.htm.

The Value of Friendship: How to Establish & Sustain a Friends Scheme (2013). Detailed, practical guidance from the Diocese of Oxford with a stress on Friends groups building community. It includes a model charity constitution and terms of reference for sub-committees with related discussion exercises. Use the search facility at www.oxford.anglican.org

A Friends Group for Your Church: A toolkit for action (2013). This easy to read resource includes a model constitution but note that a separate charity is the only option discussed. www.nationalchurchestrust.org.

Building Friends: a toolkit for new Friends groups. This helpful 2013 resource can be found using the search facility at www.london.anglican.org

4
ASSETS, EVENTS AND APPEALS

Congregations of all denominations play a significant part in caring for our nation's heritage. To illustrate the point Trevor Cooper notes that there are 15 sculptures by John Flaxman in the Victoria and Albert Museum - and a further 130 in parish churches.[36] Again, as we have noted, churches and their auxiliary buildings are used for a range of community services and activities. And, of course, the public worship and pastoral ministry of our churches is readily available to all.

Treasurers and trustees know all too well that none of these things come cheap. As stewards of our national heritage and of the good will and expectations of many in our communities it is right that churches should, where possible, draw income from their buildings, from grants to assist in caring for them and the day to day use that our communities make of them.

In this chapter we consider how we can maximise our income from the physical assets which the church has and from the support and affection that our churches receive from the wider community.

A word to the wise

Before we set off, a few brief words of caution. However welcome these related income streams may be they are rarely the silver bullet to slay our financial fears. For the Church of England just 7% of total recurring income in 2012 came from fundraising activities and 12% from trading. However, there are costs attached to these income streams and when those costs are considered the net income reduces to 6% for fundraising and 6% for trading.

Second, these income streams are more vulnerable than regular giving. Rental income can be hit hard when a new community centre is built or when key users pull out or where a 'guest congregation' from another denomination move on. Meanwhile, fundraising events depend on people's time and energy and this can be in short supply.

Finally, beware of inadvertently creating or sustaining a 'fundraising culture' which privileges fundraising over committed direct giving, subtly creating the illusion that we are all doing our bit. Both new and existing

---

[36] *Keeping our parish churches: further thoughts*, Ecclesiology Today 40 (2008) page 96.

church members can subliminally catch the idea that a familiar diet of fairs, sales and sponsored events is how we support our church financially. Like tributaries to the Mersey these income streams *complement* direct giving, they don't replace it. And just as the banks of a river give the water its force so planning and managing our income from assets and activities helps us get the best from them and not lose something important in the process.

Trading income

Trading income is simply the catch-all term for money generated from church property and from church activities. Make the most of the tangible assets you have: the church building, maybe a church hall and its rental possibilities, a car park or possibly residential property and the various activities that you or third parties host.

It is worth making three quick points. First, most registered charities and churches must return financial accounts which record trading income and the associated costs of that trading; this is good practice even where churches are not registered charities. Second, this is a helpful income stream. Churches on average rent out their assets for around 70 hours per month which produces a guesstimated average income between £8,500 and £11,600 per year.[37] Third, these assets have been entrusted to us and it is good stewardship to make the best of them. So, don't be nervous of or feel guilty about trying to increase income from your trading activities.

Realistic rents

Churches sometimes struggle here because affordable rents are one way to serve our community. So we hesitate to charge realistic rents and sometimes don't charge on principle. Some arrangements are years old and hard to unravel without creating tension and in fairness some church facilities are limited and charges should reflect what we offer. But don't be a soft touch! There are stories of churches receiving peppercorn rents from profit making enterprises or not getting a fair rent from voluntary organisations.

Trustees have an obligation under charity law to maximise their income. We can only charge reduced rents if the use is consistent with the charitable purpose of the church. So there can and will be a difference between rental costs for church organisations and local charitable groups sharing our aims and what we charge external groups making a charge for services or offering a definite benefit to their members.

---

[37] The National Churches Trust Survey 2011 page 41.

Review all rents regularly and make it clear to organisations and individuals that this is what you will do. Putting some organisations on long notice can help.

Proper paperwork

Get the paperwork right upstream and avoid problems downstream. Distinguish between *casual* lettings such as the Boys' Brigade on Monday evenings and *formal* lettings which effectively guarantee an exclusive time and day to, for example, a fee paying toddler group. The latter will need a formal written agreement. Put in writing any reduced rent to organisations whose aims are similar to your own. If you lease your buildings you must obtain best value and the Charity Commission require a Section 119 report by a competent person. If in any doubt take professional advice.

Anyone using your premises must abide by the church safeguarding policy which must, of course, be adequate and up to date.

Creativity counts

Ambleside Parish Church in the Lake District generates regular income from a few established private parking spaces on land which for years sat empty and unnoticed. St Luke's Walton sits cosily in the corner of Goodison Park and is a great place for a pre-match cuppa. The converted Baptist chapel at Hawkshead Hill in the Lake District, with origins dating to 1678, extends hospitality to tourists and walkers, offers a bedroom for retreats and a poustinia for personal reflection. St Mary and St Anne in Birmingham have converted their former parish rooms into residential accommodation and fitted solar panels to the roof of St Mary's which now generate a regular income from the feed-in-tariff. St John, Saxmundham has sensitively installed a kitchen in the south aisle of the listed church facilitating the use of the church building for concerts and recitals and a business breakfast as well as transforming the after service experience on a Sunday. The award winning St Peter's Centre at Peterchurch near Hereford now hosts a café, a branch library, luncheon club, event venue and much more. The beautifully redesigned nave hosts community activities while also remaining a place of worship.

These are just a few examples of the creative things churches are doing around the country to enhance their ministry and often, but not always, to increase income. Many have sought grant funding to improve their facilities, increasing access, usage and rental. So ask yourselves...

- Do you need to enhance the facilities that you have in order to make them more attractive to potential users?
- Do you need some external advice on possible funding applications to improve facilities – and advice on what is possible and permissible in a listed building?
- Do you need professional advice on selling or developing property?
- Do you need to talk to the gatekeepers in your community in the voluntary and statutory sectors about their needs and how you might be able to meet them?

Transparent trustees

Ask the question now and save tears later: who gets the money? In some churches the church hall income may be held in a separate bank account and a hall committee, who do a remarkable job of maintaining the hall, decide upon a *donation* to the church. In fact the hall income belongs to the general fund of the church and other internal arrangements should provide for the upkeep of the hall.

Fundraising events

Congregations are past masters at fundraising, endlessly creative and committed to give their time and energy as well as their money. From coffee mornings, jumble sales and summer fairs to sponsored abseils, charity auctions, classy dinner parties and walks up Kilimanjaro, churches have done the lot.[38]

A wonderful episode of *The Vicar of Dibley* features Kylie Minogue opening the village fete. It captures well the important truth that fundraising events are not just about money. They help build the social life of a church and its wider community and build a strong and positive public profile for the church. Fundraising events can be stepping stones for some to get more involved in church life while others want to simply play their part in supporting their church. There are lots of good things to be said for fundraising events and they should be part of the income of every church.

But, as you know, there can be a downside. Fundraising events can involve a great deal of time and effort to raise what can sometimes be relatively small amounts of money and the burden falls on a dwindling number of active people. Here are a few practical suggestions.

---

[38] A handy collection of ideas for church fundraising alongside others can be found at www.better-fundraising-ideas.com/church-fundraising.html

First, *set yourselves a realistic fundraising target.* This gives you a goal to aim at, a milestone for celebration and, crucially, permission to slow down or even stop when you have hit the target. Be realistic about the time, energy and people available. If the summer fair committee is a year older and fewer in number we set ourselves up to fail if we plan for a 20% increase on last year. But if the church is celebrating a special anniversary then set a more ambitious target.

Second, *set a funding event strategy and timetable.* Plan the key fundraising activities in advance. Some will be a given, a Christmas Fair or the Harvest charity auction. Others can be planned around fixed points in the church diary. This way you avoid bunching events and the demands on people's energy and pockets and you can turn down or delay the great new funding opportunity that someone enthusiastically commends.

Third, *set the ethical boundaries for your fundraising.* This is a bigger issue in some churches than others and for some individuals more than others. Align your values and your fundraising. A church policy is helpful to politely turn down the offer of tarot readings at the Christmas fair. A quick check of the second hand book stall may pull several books you may not expect to pick up in church! Individuals may not gamble or drink so be sensitive about those raffle tickets for 12 bottles of France's finest. People choose their own socialising so not participating in a fundraising event doesn't necessarily mean lack of commitment.

Fourth, *set yourselves up for the digital world.* We'll look at this a little more in the next chapter. Here we just note that online giving platforms can power donations to sponsored events while social media can help promote and profile your event.

Finally, *set out to keep the fun in fundraising.* One vicar told me that unless the Christmas fair hit £6,000 the church would be in big trouble. There is not much fun in that kind of fundraising. When the financial target becomes the be all and end all of the event we have lost something very special.

Appeals

200 years old in 2014, St George's Church in Everton is Grade 1 listed and the world's first iron church. They needed £267,000 to repair the roof and preserve the fabric. The Heritage Lottery Fund came up trumps but a shortfall of £53,000 is a huge ask for a parish amongst the 1% most

deprived parishes in England.[39]

St George's is by no means alone. The same story is told across the UK and in all denominations. Incredibly congregations absorb something like 85% of the cost of routine repairs to church buildings. Inevitably, however, major repairs come around and when these exceed £50,000 churches absorb around two thirds of the cost and have to find the rest from somewhere.[40] And although it often feels like it, church maintenance is not the only reason churches need big money. We might refurbish our church hall for community use or recruit a family or youth worker.

We launch an appeal when we are looking for *time limited, high value* money for a *specific purpose*. This is money we cannot find by adjusting our operational budget. We need a lot and we need it pretty quickly. We can appeal to grant making trusts, to major donors, to statutory bodies and to our congregations and communities.

There are excellent written resources available plus high quality advice and support from denominational bodies and from professional fundraisers. See the Resources section for some places to start. Here I offer a brief overview of some key points.

The beat of a different drum

First, a capital appeal has a different dynamic to the nurture of planned giving. The goal is to get the most money from the fewest people in the shortest time. A capital appeal is more exposed, more public and more risky. It requires some high octane local leadership, not least in modelling the giving we hope for from other people. It requires time, energy and commitment and we cannot avoid 'the ask'. Churches have to manage this dynamic while not compromising that regular giving.

Win the war on paper first

Don't rush into battle. Don't go public with your appeal until you know where the money is coming from and when a good chunk of the money is already secured. Avoid what I heard one fundraiser call, 'spray and pray': spraying out letters and praying someone will give money! There's a time for launches, letters and fundraising activities but get your funding strategy on paper first, praying as you go. Professional fundraisers will conduct an

---

[39] In passing, remember that for listed churches VAT can be reclaimed on eligible works. See the guidance at www.lpwscheme.org.uk
[40] The National Churches Trust Survey (2011) page 50.

intensive research or resources study of how people feel about the project and where money is likely to come from.

Win hearts and minds first by drafting your case for support. This is what Simon George calls, 'the generic sales document that sets out why your work deserves to be funded, identifies the benefits it will deliver and makes a compelling case for the funds you need, the reason why anyone would give you money'.[41] I remember one fundraiser reading the case statement of a church project and simply observing that there was not £350,000 of benefit in the proposal. The need alone does not make the case for support. You must answer the 'so what?' challenge. 'The old minibus is finished – so what?' Answer: the new one will help us tackle elderly and youth isolation in remote rural communities.

Next, logistics: know how you will raise the money before you start to raise it. Map out the various sources of money available to you and their relative importance. One or two will be your lead gifts, those 'make or break' gifts that determine the success of the project. What other grants may be possible? Which small trusts can you approach to finish the job? What can you raise from the committed members of the church? How much will fundraising activities reasonably bring in? A community project will open up more grant making trusts than a project for mainly congregational benefit but do research the trusts properly.

Step by step

Every appeal has a number of stages; cover the bases at each stage before moving on. The first stage is the planning and you will need a planning group that is big enough and has the right skills for the task in hand. You may find willing help outside of the congregation so don't be afraid to ask. Prepare the case for support, the funding plan and any promotional literature.

Next secure those critical first gifts. In a church context this can have two elements. The first is that big gift, often a key grant making trust but it may be a legacy or a gift from a major donor. The lead gift or gifts should hit at least 10%-15% of the total needed. The second element is the pledges of the appeal or campaign committee and the wider leadership of the church. In monetary terms this may well be less than a large grant but the value of these pledges is to demonstrate the commitment of those

---

[41] Raising Funds from Grant Makers: how to make successful applications to grant making bodies by Simon George (SPM Fundessentials, 2012) page 23.

closest to the project which will underwrite all your subsequent requests for support. Note that I say 'pledges' here. While some can give lump sum gifts many more will pledge regular gifts over a four or five year period.

At this point we are still under the radar but with at least 25% of the total secured, ideally up to 40% or more. *Now* we go public. Launch the appeal in the wider congregation seeking *their* pledges. Contact the wider public, former church members, the Friends group. Start that second phase of applications to grant making trusts and get cracking on those fund raising activities. Finally there is a period of what we might call consolidation. Most of the money is in but we still need to finish the job. Here we approach those small trusts who can help us with a small grant, or put an article in the local paper saying how close we are to our target or approach one or two individuals to help finish the job.

Sources of funding

The resources at the end of this chapter cover this subject in detail so the briefest of comments here. Look to any church reserves; this *is* the rainy day and no one will give you money to save you spending your own. Never underestimate the high accumulated value of regular gifts over four or five years. 50 people giving just £2 a week for five years is £26,000 plus any Gift Aid. Many will give more than £2 if you ask them. Grant making trusts and community foundations are benevolent organisations. They want to make a difference but you must meet their criteria; do your research, make your case and make the ask. Trusts come in sizes large and small so consider *what* you ask for and *when* in the life cycle of your appeal. Major donors, those wealthy individuals who can make a significant gift, are out there but you have to find them, make your case and ask them.

Your fundraising activities can make a difference when accumulated over time. Many will be relatively small and offer awareness value as much as they make money. Some, however, can be really valuable; events such as dinners and charity auctions might raise five figure sums. Raising money from local businesses is always possible but without care can be a source of disappointment. They are businesses not charities and an offer which includes a degree of recognition and publicity plus a sense of contributing to community is important.

Gift Days

A hefty Heritage Lottery Fund grant still left St James' Birkdale, home of those famous golf links, short of £100,000 to repair the church spire. At St James' an annual review focusing on regular giving is complemented by a November Gift Day, sometimes dealing with budget shortfalls, sometimes focusing on specific projects.

For the spire project timing was difficult; all churches know the feeling! The Gift Day needed to address a budget shortfall and on the same day after the morning service a meeting addressed the spire project. An appeal leaflet and congregational letters made the ask and a Saturday was set apart as day of prayer. Remarkably within three months both the budget shortfall and the spire project were funded.

Now a Gift Day cannot short circuit the careful planning and visible leadership of a capital appeal but it can be an excellent way to focus the appeal for the congregation. By including project information, guidance on how and how much to give, communicating thanks and making prayer a priority a Gift Day can also help to model good financial stewardship.

Gift Days do tend to work best as occasional events linked to a specific appeal but St James' is by no means alone in having a Gift Day to address operational deficits. A carefully planned Gift Day can be part of the stewardship architecture of the church and may serve as the focus of the annual review touched on in chapter one. In more rural churches it can be a focus for regular support from the wider community. However, do beware of putting a sticking plaster over a problem year on year as it can divert regular income as people become accustomed to retain giving for the Gift Day.[42]

Conclusion

Churches have inherited a wide range of physical assets and it is good trusteeship and good stewardship practice to make the best of those assets where we can. Many are also blessed with people who give their time and energy, both in the congregation and the wider community. Careful planning of fundraising and appeals will honour, protect and maximise the effectiveness of all our supporters who are able and willing to give.

---

[42] For good practical advice on Gift Days see *Giving for the Glory of God* at www.parishresources.org.uk/giving

Resources

Raising Funds from Grant Makers, Simon George (SPM Fundessentials, 2012). A concise and comprehensive guide by the director of Wootton George Consulting.

The UK Church Fundraising Handbook, Maggie Durran (Canterbury Press 2003). A comprehensive book aimed at churches and weighted towards capital projects with detailed guidance on the tools and processes needed for church appeals

Faith Based Fundraising: handy toolkits from the Church Urban Fund at www.cuf.org.uk/near-neighbours/resources

Fundraising for Small Charities, James Myers (SPM Fundessentials, 2011). A small book covering much ground, aimed at small charities with much that is suggestive for churches.

Capital fundraising in the UK – The Compton Way. This book offers guidance on a capital campaign from UK fundraising consultancy Compton International with much experience of working with churches. (www. comptonfundraising.co.uk)

Craigmyle Fundraising Consultants (www.craigmyle.org.uk): professional fundraising consultancy, again with extensive experience of working with churches to raise capital funds.

5
THERE'S AN APP FOR THAT: DIGITAL GIVING

I heard former Archbishop of Canterbury, George Carey, tell the following story. A narrow gauge railway train is chugging along slowly. A man starts trotting alongside the train and soon reaches the front. He asks the engine driver if he can go faster. 'I can', replies the driver, 'but I have to stay with the train'.

Internet technology and culture is changing how we give to charity. Digital giving or online fundraising, call it what you will, is here to stay and rich with possibilities. However, churches, like charities, have to work out the best way of capitalising on these opportunities.

So as we set out, again just a few words of caution. First, just having an online presence is not enough. Even in a digital age good giving still means good asking and churches need to learn how to make a confident digital ask. Second, while digital giving is growing fast traditional giving still matters. People still post cheques and make telephone donations to charity and give to their church by weekly envelopes and standing orders so we are looking at a mixed economy and multi channel giving options. Third, remember that churches have what charities want: a personal relationship with most of their donors, so digital giving and social media should build upon and enhance the relationships we already have. Fourthly, the focus of much online giving is the one-off gift, the response to a particular need. However generous such gifts are churches will always depend on that bedrock of regular, planned giving.

Finally, in the digital world things are changing fast and as churches explore digital giving there will be more questions than answers, more possibilities to explore than solutions to apply. We may feel overwhelmed, excited or unsure where to start but remember that we have to stay with the train. Some larger churches will be able to drive digital giving hard; for the rest of us: *we cannot do everything but we can do something.*

Online giving to charity

The internet is not only changing how we live; it is itself constantly changing. At the start of 2014 over three quarters of adults (77%) had broadband internet access and nine in ten adults have a mobile phone with over half (57%) using their phone to access the internet. Over four in ten households (44%) have a tablet which has cross generational appeal, while six in ten adults now own a smartphone but much more so among younger adults than the over 65s (just 14%). Nearly half of us use social media and we now spend more time using media or communications than we do sleeping![43]

Twenty years ago a sponsored event meant chasing people with a pen and paper. Today it is likely to mean online sponsorship powered by social media and with Gift Aid built in. The Bristol based Love Running initiative grew out of a single church and using an online giving platform, email and social media has raised nearly £500,000 through people running for good causes.

In just ten years JustGiving, the best known digital giving platform, has facilitated £1.5 billion of charitable giving. In January 2014 around 57% of JustGiving traffic was mobile via phones and tablets compared to just 4% in 2010.[44] On average 40% say that online giving is or will be our main way of giving to charity and the figure is higher for those aged 18-24 (53%) and aged 25-34 (63%).[45]

Blackbaud UK report that most charities now accept online donations and note that online giving increased by 85% between 2008 and 2011. Charities receive on average 15% of all individual donations from online donations but there is considerable variation with a third of charities receiving less than 5% online. 55% of survey respondents reported an increase in online giving between 2013 and 2014. The challenge for charities seems now to be their *mobile* strategy.[46]

Social media is helping to drive charitable giving and is used by charities to communicate with their supporters. One survey of 8,000 online donors found that a friend or family member asking for sponsorship online was the main reason for donations while social media was next with 30% claiming that social media inspired their giving although few will use social media to actually make their gift.[47] Social media matters on two counts. First, when people share their giving stories on social media it helps grow

[43] The Communications Market Report: United Kingdom accessed at media.ofcom.org.uk/facts
[44] Going Mobile, Being Social. Institute of Fundraising presentation July 2014 accessed at www.slideshare.net/justgiving
[45] Blackbaud UK: The Psychology of Online Giving page 2. Access at www.blackbaud.co.uk
[46] Blackbaud UK: State of the Not for Profit Industry 2014. Access at www.blackbaud.co.uk. The data is consistent with the 2013 survey. Digital Donor Review 2013 (infographic) at www.giveasyoulive.com/digitaldonorreview)
[47] Digital Donor Review 2012 page 26 and page 33.

a culture of giving. Second, social media empowers our friends to do the telling and asking on our behalf. They become our advocates and our champions.

Doing what we can

Don't forget that the humble standing order and direct debit are forms of digital giving but so commonplace and trusted we barely give them a thought. As we all become more confident in the security of our personal data and as developments such as mobile payments become normalised and familiar digital giving will become more significant. As things stand there are good things we can do now and much to watch with interest for future developments. It is a mistake to think that older people don't do digital and younger people don't read emails or visit websites. Digital giving is and must be blended into our funding strategy in the church alongside traditional ways of giving and communicating.

What we do must be *fruitful* in its results, it must be *sustainable* given our resources of people, time and money, it must be *integrated* into our overall communications and it must be *done well*. The challenge is not to do everything but to be open to the possibilities. For example, a new Messy Church initiative has a Facebook page with five younger volunteers regularly adding stories and pictures. It's proving a hit with parents and children and includes an invitation to give via a link to a donations page on the church website.

Two challenges and an opportunity

Something around half of regular church giving is in the hands of those over 65[48] so we face the challenge of creating a culture of giving amongst our younger church members. Given that younger people engage more with social media and are comfortable with online giving these developments may offer us tools which can help younger adults in the practice of generosity.

As noted above, however, digital giving especially enhances those one-off gifts to charity and church: those special appeals, the sponsored events, the micro donations via text giving. As one report comments, 'the challenge for fundraisers in the UK is translating smaller gift amount mobile giving into longer term, more profitable forms of giving such as becoming

---

[48] See the indicative research in *Giving Insight* pages 9-10; details in the Resources section of Chapter 2 which is consistent with our own findings in the Diocese of Liverpool.

a regular monthly donor'.[49] This second challenge is no less pressing for churches: the complex task of translating one off gifts into regular planned giving. Churches may well be able to learn much from the wider charitable sector.

Intriguingly some online giving platforms are now facilitating regular giving while regular text giving is also a possibility. On these digital giving options more is said below. This is an important but longer term investment for the church but, as noted above, there are more hard questions than easy answers.

First steps in a digital world
Practically speaking then, what can churches do to take some first steps into the age of digital giving?

The church website
Don't get in a twist about Twitter; a well designed, visual and up to date website will require a budget and time but is not a big ask.[50]

People visit websites looking for information so it must be there. But your website should always tell a story about your vision, the difference you make. As one report on online giving says, 'visit even the biggest charities' websites and often the need to persuade is forgotten.' Younger donors are more likely to visit a charity website before making a gift than older givers but all donors most frequently report visiting a website as a way to keep in touch with their charities.[51]

Online giving platforms, on which see below, make it easy to have a donations button; do you have one? It should be easy to find; is yours? Remember, older people are quite as comfortable as their young counterparts with making online donations.[52]

Increasingly we access the internet via our mobile phone and while a mobile friendly website may be a step too far for many churches it is worth ensuring that at least your home page and donations page are mobile friendly.

---

[49] The Next Generation of Giving in the UK 2013 page 4. See the Resources section for details.
[50] To make a start on a church website visit www.churchedit.co.uk.
[51] The quote is from, Passion, persistence, and partnership: the secrets of earning more online. *nfpSynergy 2011 page 6.* See also The Next Generation of Giving page 8.
[52] Next Generation of UK Giving page 5.

Email

Email is significant, especially for older online users but still with a cross generational appeal if donors are familiar with the cause. Collect email addresses but use this database strategically, not to exhaustively promote every church activity in isolation from your other communications. Use email to communicate achievements and exciting initiatives. Keep them brief and punchy and email newsletters of a good quality if you want people to read them. Segment your email lists so that what goes to the regular congregation is different from your communications with former or distant members who stay in touch from afar.

Digital giving platforms

As I write two friends are running a half marathon for charity and a third is sleeping on the roof of her church - to raise money for the church roof appeal! Like thousands of others they are using a digital giving platform to tell their story, receive donations and to inform about online and offline money raised. Their friends are finding out through Facebook and Twitter, making their donations, expressing support and perhaps telling their friends all about it also.

Giving platforms such as *MyDonate, JustGiving, Virgin Money Giving, Givey* and *give.net* from Christian charity Stewardship make it easy for churches to create fundraising pages and a digital presence which supporters can talk about in social media. Churches not registered with the Charity Commission in England and Wales or with OSCR in Scotland can reclaim Gift Aid on these platforms if they are registered with HMRC for Gift Aid. Do your research; online giving platforms vary with regard to charges on each gift transaction and there may be charges to register or to host charity webpages.[53]

Crowdfunding

A small charity used popular crowdfunding website *indiegogo.com* to raise £5,000 for a water project in Kenya. The project page held a simple video, the story, the financial target and the project closing date. My friend Pete asked for my support early doors but I did my bit when his final email said they needed £450 in eight days. Meanwhile I learned from Radio 4 that an

---

[53] A handy overview of platforms and charges is TV money guru Martin Lewis' site www.moneysavingexpert.com/family/charity-fundraising-sites. Note also the new Donate platform from www.nationalfundingscheme.org which may be of interest to 'heritage churches'.

old bakery had reopened as a community bakery, crowdfunded to the tune of £19,000 (they asked for £13,000) by 500 people, including someone from Alaska.[54]

If it sounds familiar that is because the digital giving platforms we have considered are part of the crowdfunding family but there are other crowdfunding models with distinctive characteristics.

Crowdfunding platforms vary in the details but require a project target, say £4,000, and allow between 30 days to ten weeks to reach it. To add spice a fee is charged, 5% is typical, but if you only raise £3,000 you get nothing at all and no money is taken from your donors. Some sites offer flexible fees allowing you to get the £3,000 but pay a higher fee, say 9%. Some crowdfunding platforms offer donor rewards in proportion to the gift – certificates, signed photographs and much more.

The key to crowdfunding is a specific and compelling project, realistic, achievable targets, a sense of urgency and the need to be creative. Developing a crowdfunding project can do wonders to focus the thinking and creativity of a funding group. Crowdfunding is not just for charitable purposes and may suit a church when an activity is church related but not charitable or when the funding strategy includes donor benefits which disqualify donations from Gift Aid.[55]

Text giving

As one congregation left their church at the end of the morning service another, noticeably younger one, was coming in for a child's baptism, all armed to the teeth with mobile phones. Could we do more than pass a collection plate? Another church thinks so.

Here the vicar began a wedding by asking people to *mute* their mobile phones; they would need them later. After an excellent service he invited people to reset their phones and, if they wished, mark the occasion by texting a gift, say £5, to a five digit text number with a simple church code, e.g. AAAA12 £5.

Vodafone's welcome support for JustTextGiving enables churches to embrace text giving at no cost to the church or the donor. The gift is added

---

[54] Women's Hour Tuesday August 5th 2014.

[55] In the UK www.yimby.com from the Just Giving stable is a good place to start with simple guidance on crowdfunding local projects and no rewards. www.crowdfunder.co.uk is a rewards based platform. Gift Aid is not built in but can be claimed by the charity where eligible, including observance of the Gift Aid benefit rules. See www.crowdfunder.co.uk/blog/2014/09/top-tips-crowdfunding-charities and the Gift Aid guidance in chapter 7.

to the donor's monthly mobile bill and the service includes the reclaim of Gift Aid.[56]

The text function is familiar and used for a range of purposes from competitions to arranging deliveries. For charitable donations it an immediate, impulsive way to give when asked or when emotions are touched. A growing percentage of donors are now aware of and use text giving. It has a particular appeal to younger donors and nearly three quarters of UK charities (69%) use or plan to use text giving to drive donations.[57]

Text giving is no substitute for regular congregational giving but is rich in potential for one off donations: tourists or special services such as baptisms or church weddings.[58] It reduces admin on those small gifts or 'micro donations' but more crucially, with the average text donation at £3.70, text giving undermines that small change mentality which sees so much loose change in offering baskets after occasional services.[59]

The headline numbers are impressive. The 2009 Haiti earthquake appeal raised $2 million in 24 hours; Sport Relief 2012 raised £7.9 million from text giving while the remarkable Stephen Sutton inspired millions and raised £5 million for the Teenage Cancer Trust with at least £1.5 million from text giving. JustTextGiving has generated over £10 million for around 15,000 charities, an average of around £650 per charity, so can smaller charities raise serious money without big publicity?

There is a gap between the potential for text giving and the reality. Just 4% of charities record great success with text giving and 21% have tried with little success.[60] The experience of many churches seems to support this conclusion. Churches should be seeing better results than we are so two brief comments.

First, as we have already noted good giving always means good asking and our vicar at the wedding did just this. Clergy must learn to make a confident 'digital ask' as there is no fundamental difference between

---

[56] www.justgiving.com/en/justtextgiving. The basic package is a single text code and is entirely free. An unlimited package with a monthly fee offers multiple codes and donation pages.

[57] The Digital Donor Review 2013 suggests 11% make SMS donations, up from 9% in 2012. *Sending out an SMS* (see the Resources section for details) suggests 15% made a text donation in 2011 but the 2012 CAF/NCVO survey of giving indicates just 2% while 7% is given in *Embracing the 21st century – charitable giving and technology,* Sally Panayiotou, Ipsos MORI, July, 2012. The 69% figure is from Blackbaud State of the Non Profit Industry 2014 page 9. 35% of those aged 16-24 and 34% of those aged 25-34 are very or quite likely to donate via text according to *Sending out an SMS* page 33.

[58] Some text giving services facilitate *regular* text gifts including the facility to skip a regular payment and over time this may be a development to watch. (www.cymba.co.uk/regular_text_giving.php)

[59] *Sending out an SMS*: page 36.

[60] *Sending out an SMS* page 40; Digital Donor Review 2013 suggests that three quarters of charities are not using text to fundraise.

inviting cash on a plate or a text gift from a phone. Second, text giving is immediate, impulsive, triggered by emotion and experience so word your ask to key into that: 'if you would like to thank God for...'; or, 'if you would like to celebrate this special day... you can make a gift by texting...'.

Mobile giving

Of course text giving is done by mobile phone but what I have in mind here is the technology that links bank accounts with mobile phone numbers and email addresses and facilitates mobile payments and, by extension, charity donations via a smartphone app. Over 28 million people manage their bank accounts online and mobile payments is an emerging technology.[61]

Currently for all but the largest churches, however, mobile giving is one to watch because there are hurdles to clear. First mobile giving must piggyback growing public familiarity with and confidence in the security of mobile payments coupled with ease of use in one's hand.

Second, the technology that underwrites both familiarity and confidence is still emerging. Paym, launched by the banking industry in April 2014 and integrated within proprietary banking apps is a database linking mobile phone numbers to bank accounts. It will facilitate peer to peer and limited business transactions with the promise of serving 90% of current account holders by the end of 2014. Already a huge player PayPal enables account holders to make mobile payments to contacts, to make online and increasingly in-store purchases and has the capacity to link bank accounts and plastic to the PayPal account.[62] The inclusion within iPhone 6 of Apple Pay, a mobile payments system with 'one touch checkout' may well help to mainstream mobile payments.[63] When paying by mobile is normalised it could be a game changer for charitable giving.

Third, there are technical details around adapting personal mobile payment models to charitable giving while one report identifies three key issues for charities: claiming Gift Aid, capturing donor details and more generically, ease of use.[64] Ahead of the field is Barclay's Pingit, a giving

---

[61] 85% of respondents in a banking industry survey thought that person-to-person and person-to-business mobile payments would be a mainstream option within five years with half believing it would happen in two. *The Changing Face of Payments* (2014) page 29. Accessed via www.vocalink.com

[62] www.paym.co.uk; www.paypal.com/uk/home

[63] This is a western perspective. In Kenya high mobile ownership, remote rural communities and lack of access to banking infrastructure has made mobile payments common place through the money service M-Pesa. The MasterCard Mobile Payments Readiness Index rates Kenya at 40.4, the UK at 37.5 with Singapore top at 45.6. A score of 60 marks the point "at which mobile devices account for an appreciable share of the payments mix". http://mobilereadiness.mastercard.com

[64] Using Mobile Payments to drive Charitable Donations; accessed at www.vocalink.com

channel used by Children in Need; making a gift using the Pingit app and QR code is both quick and easy. Pingit facilitates but does not reclaim Gift Aid and is certainly one to watch.

'Click and Give' websites

This form of fundraising, built around online shopping and web searching, has potential for churches because gifts can be made in the background and at no additional cost to the donor or the church. It is, as one site is named, 'Give as you Live' and this platform alone has generated nearly £5 million for charitable causes.[65]

A church must register itself with a 'click and give' website to receive donations. The process is simple requiring either a charity number or the HMRC reference number, showing the church is a charity for tax purposes. Individuals must also register with the site and choose their church from the charity list so that donations can be made as they shop. Next, start shopping at thousands of online stores and each purchase triggers a donation of a percentage of your purchase to the church, at no extra cost to you.

'Click and give' is simple to set up, easy to use and because internet shopping is here to stay is potentially rewarding for churches. Promote it carefully, perhaps starting with a small group, a home group for example, who can champion the idea in the congregation. As ever, remember this is part of a balanced fundraising scorecard. Don't appear desperate to try anything and remember that some are reluctant to shop online out of security concerns or the impact on jobs and the high street.

eBay for charity

Charity auctions have long been a way of raising funds and they can be held online. Anyone selling on eBay can choose to donate a percentage to the charity of their choice. It is also possible for the church to host a special auction on eBay with supporters donating items and the money raised going direct to the church.[66]

Conclusion

A church prays one Sunday for a small team visiting a partner church in Rwanda. The church magazine tells the story as does a visual web page

---

[65] www.giveasyoulive.com; www.easyfundraising.org.uk; www.givingabit.com
[66] pages.ebay.co.uk/ebayforcharity/specialauctions.html

which also carries a Twitter feed and a team member blog. One blog graphically describes the local maternity ward, also filmed by another team member on her mobile. The video is posted on YouTube, the church website and a digital giving page which asks for £5,000 to buy new equipment and redecorate. An email is sent to church members and contacts in the local Rotary club while several members add it to their Facebook and Twitter accounts. The £5,000 is there before the team arrive back in the UK.

It is of course never quite that smooth in reality, but digital giving and social media do offer creative takes on traditional way to fundraise and new possibilities. The challenge is to be as creative as you can within your means, make sure that what you do is sustainable and above all be consistent and confident in making that digital ask.

Resources

Sending out an SMS: The potential of mobile phones for charities and non-profits; a report from nfpSynergy and Charities Aid Foundation (2nd edition June 2011).

Passion, persistence, and partnership: the secrets of earning more online (Mission Fish, CAF, nfpSynergy and IoF; 2nd Edition 2011). A useful overview of digital giving, accessed at nfpsynergy.net

The Next Generation of Giving in the UK 2013: Insights into generational giving and the importance of a multi-channel approach to approaching donors. Access at www.blackbaud.co.uk

More than shaking an online tin: How can we take technology-enabled giving to a new level? (May 2012). Access at www.nominettrust.org.uk/knowledge-centre/resources

Crowding In: How the UK's businesses, charities, government, and financial system can make the most of crowdfunding. Accessed at www.nesta.org.uk (December 2012). A readable short guide to crowdfunding models and future potential.

Crowdfunding: the wisdom and wallets of crowds. A useful introduction to Crowdfunding. Access at www.nominettrust.org.uk/knowledge-centre/resources

6
A GIFT OF LIFE: THE VALUE OF LEGACIES

A lay leader, personally convinced of the importance of legacy income, raised the issue of promoting gifts in wills at a church well situated in and well loved by its community. There was some anxiety that the church may lose the goodwill that had generated legacy gifts in the past, and his suggestion was not followed.

Elsewhere a clergyman was perplexed that a faithful church member had bequeathed a six figure legacy, not to the church that had nurtured faith for some fifty years but to a national charity which would, of course, have used it well but with which there seemed to be no prior connection. Is it because, as a member of another church put it, 'we just don't think about the church like that'?

Anxiety surrounds the issue but legacy giving is the single, largest missed opportunity for churches to grow income and resource ministry and mission.

The church has a huge giving base of regular, committed, planned givers. There is no practical or theological reason why this generous giving should be limited only to our disposable income or constrained by our death. Outside our congregations a legacy is one way in which people choose to express affection and goodwill to their local church. Add to this the age profile of many congregations and we should be seeing more legacy income than we do.

According to Christian Legacy, 'our research shows that many church-goers are open to the idea of leaving a Christian legacy – if only someone would suggest it, and help them take the first steps'. The challenge for the church is that charities are doing the asking. The same 2009 research found that while 85% of Christians heard about legacy giving from charities just 18% heard legacy teaching in their church, a figure which had happily grown to 23% by 2013 but is still way too low.[67]

Every church, large and small, can encourage will making and gifts in wills as a normal part of stewardship thinking and practice.

---

[67] www.christianlegacy.org.uk. In 2013 by contrast 60% of respondents were taught by their church about tithing and 86% about regular giving.

The value of gifts in wills

Legacies are worth more than £2 billion a year to charities representing around 5% of total income of charities and 13% of voluntary income. Sustained growth in the value of legacies stalled in the aftermath of the financial crisis of 2008 and in real terms values decreased by 9% between 2008 and 2012.

However, the market is recovering as the number and value of bequests grows, the value driven largely by an increase in house prices while the general economic outlook improves. By 2018 legacies should be worth around £2.7 billion, although this represents rather less growth in real terms.[68]

Longer term, the next 30 or so years will see a rising death rate and the passing of the more affluent, charitably minded Boomer generation. On current trends by 2030 the projected increase in the death rate alone will result in an additional 22,500 legacies. Growth will be due to the number of legacies as well as their value as it is estimated that charitable bequests will double, the percentage of wills including a legacy will rise from 14% to 19% and that by 2050 in real terms legacies will be worth around £5.2 billion.[69]

Now today's £2 billion is a lot of money which does a lot of good and amazingly comes from relatively few legacy gifts. Between 6% and 7% of those who die leave a will with a charitable legacy with an average of three gifts per will.[70] In times past, says legacy expert Claire Routley, legacy gifts were quite normal. Indeed a plaque in Durham Cathedral says this of a man known as a 'fortress of the poor':

> *But why, you ask, leaves he no legacies?*
> *Why break this generous habit when he dies?*
> *The reason's plain: he had given when alive*
> *So largely that he had no more to give*
> *He lodged his all with Christ, this merchant wise.*
> *That calm might be his journey to the skies.*[71]

[68] Legacy Market Snapshot 2014. The papers referenced in this chapter, the Legacy Matters newsletter; a quarterly Legacy Bulletin and an annual Legacy Market Snapshot are freely available from www.legacyforesight.co.uk, an excellent source of legacy statistics and insights in a field where the numbers change fast. A useful presentation by Meg Abdy of Legacy Foresight is *Legacy market outlook - living with the 'new normal'* (13th September 2013) access at www.institute-of-fundraising.org.uk/library

[69] Legacy Matters Autumn 2011; Legacy Matters Spring 2014.

[70] Legacy Market Snapshot 2013; Legacy Matters Autumn 2011.

[71] Claire drew attention to this plaque at a stewardship conference in June 2014. Her website and blog is at www.legacyfundraising.co.uk.

Although a small percentage of deaths result in a legacy gift, having a will, the likelihood of leaving a legacy and actually doing so all rise with age. An estimated 37% of adults have a will with 15% of these leaving a charitable legacy. Amongst people over 65 as we would expect a much higher figure, 63% have a will and 18% have included charitable provision. Around 40% of the adult population could be considered 'warm' prospects while amongst donors and volunteers over a third leave a legacy.[72] A step change in our attitudes, expectations and behaviour around legacies would make a huge difference to the causes we care about.

Gifts to charity are exempt from Inheritance Tax and the government is keen to 'nudge' us to greater legacy giving. Since 2012 a charitable donation of 10% of an estate (a percentage which should ring bells for Christians) results in a reduction in inheritance tax for the remainder of the estate from 40% to 36%.[73] Important initiatives such as Will Aid and Remember a Charity are helping to mainstream consideration of legacies when people make their will and support from solicitors is crucial to this.[74]

Types of legacy

It is worth noting that legacies are of different types and values. The value of the average *pecuniary* legacy, that is a gift of *cash*, fluctuates yearly but across all UK charities in 2014 was around £2,600. This average value is always skewed by a few larger pecuniary gifts so a legacy of £1,000 would not be unusual.[75] The number and the average value of these pecuniary legacies have risen since the recession.[76] Pecuniary legacies represent around 55% of all gifts but make up just 8% of legacy income.

This is because *residuary* gifts, a share or a percentage of an estate, are worth significantly more than pecuniary gifts and account for around 85% of legacy income for charities. The average residual gift has fluctuated in recent years from around £35,000 to over £50,000; in 2014 it is around £40,000 but this figure is again skewed by a small number of large gifts. A more realistic residual average is £20,000 - £25,000. A third type of

---

[72] Legacy Market Snapshot 2013 and 14. The donor and volunteer figure is from Richard Radcliffe: www.civilsociety.co.uk/fundraising/blogs/content/7248/an_uncertain_legacy.

[73] This is complex. See the Stewardship paper in the Resources section of this chapter.

[74] www.willaid.org.uk; www.rememberacharity.org.uk

[75] Legacy Market Snapshot 2014. A higher figure of £3,670 in Legacy Bulletin issue 3 2014 represents the Legacy Foresight consortium of charities. A figure of £3,167 for places of worship is offered by Smee and Ford in an Institute of Fundraising presentation dated 10 December 2013.

[76] I am indebted to Meg Abdy for the observation that this is probably due to values being set before the recession as on average a last will is written six years before death.

legacy, *specific* legacies such as jewellery, property or shares and other more complex things, make up 8% of legacy notifications and 6% of income and are higher in value than pecuniary but less than residuary gifts.[77]

Pecuniary gifts are fixed sums which can be significantly eroded by inflation over time. Residual gifts as a *share* of an estate can significantly rise in value in the same period depending, of course, on the economic situation.

Legacies and the Church

Churches already benefit hugely from legacy gifts. Legacy Foresight estimate some £240 million of legacy income went to faith based organisations and local churches.[78] In 2012 Church of England parishes received a little under £45 million of legacy income, of which £30 million was in unrestricted gifts. Legacy gifts, large and small, enable churches to do everything from buying new crockery through replacing heating systems to major repair work or employing a children's worker.[79] As we shall see, using legacies well is key to generating more legacy income.

However, the picture is patchy. Churches will reflect the regional variations in legacies in which the south east, perhaps not surprisingly, sees the most income and growth while within the legacy market the advancement of religion is one of the cause areas showing slower growth.[80] As with charities, in a given year the majority of churches receive no legacies, some get small amounts and a handful receive six figure gifts, occasionally more. If the Church of England is any guide (and the data is only suggestive, not certain) it also seems that churches tend to receive more of those lower value pecuniary legacies, perhaps 64%, compared to the charitable sector (55%) while residual church legacies represent perhaps 60% of income, less than the charitable sector equivalent (85%). When promoting legacy giving we should not shy away from residual legacies although we would never use that technical language.

In short, despite our excellent giving base the lifetime generosity of Christians is not reflected in the income churches receive from gifts in wills compared to the charitable sector. Legacy income to the Church

---

[77] Abdy: *Legacy market outlook - living with the 'new normal'*.

[78] Legacy Foresight: Spotlight on faith-based legacies July 2014. I am grateful to Meg Abdy of Legacy Foresight for this shared information.

[79] Case studies of churches blessed by legacies are on the 'amazing gifts' pages at the excellent www.churchlegacy.org.uk

[80] Legacy Matters Autumn 2013.

of England is just 7% of total voluntary income compared to 13% in the charitable sector. There is more we can do.

Taking action

So what can churches do? Doing nothing and hoping for the best just occasionally pays off. But our theology, pastoral practice and mission opportunities demand more of us than that. We can grasp this rich opportunity.

Be confident

This is where we must start. Be confident that making a will is important; an act of love and wise stewardship. It is often pointed out that the Visitation of the Sick in the 1662 Book of Common Prayer urges the preparation of a will and dealing with financial matters both for the comfort of the soul and the peace of executors.[81] The bible encourages care for one's family (1 Timothy 5:8) and an up to date will is a prudent, caring and practical way of doing just that.

Be confident also to request legacy gifts because Christians are among those warm prospects, those donors and volunteers willing to make a gift in their will. In fact nearly half of Christians have or would consider a legacy.[82] Less often quoted is the additional exhortation at the Visitation of the Sick that, 'The minister should not omit earnestly to move such sick persons as are of ability to be liberal to the poor'.

A legacy captures our passion for the church, charities and causes that matter to us in life. A legacy is a joyful, life affirming gift which can make a difference like no other gift we might make. After a lifetime of giving faithfully from our disposable *income* a legacy simply extends that same stewardship principle and practice to generous giving from our *wealth*, our whole estate.

Be willing to ask

There is no great mystery behind encouraging gifts in Wills. As Richard Radcliffe notes, legacies start with a please or a thank you. Sensitively, gently and courteously we need to invite people to think about making their will and leaving a legacy gift. Asking makes a difference. In a recent

---

[81] 'Men should often be put in remembrance to take order for the settling of their temporal estates, whilst they are in health.' (The Visitation of the Sick).
[82] Legacy Matters Autumn 2011 summarising research from the Christian Legacy Consortium.

experiment when solicitors simply mentioned that leaving a legacy was an option the percentage of people who made a gift doubled to 10%. When solicitors asked if those making a will were passionate about any charities the percentage increased to 15% and the value of gifts increased by 50%. [83]

Be positive

'Welcome to the joyful world of legacy giving' says Richard Radcliffe, noting that legacy gifts are driven by life and only activated by death.[84] A legacy is a joyful, life affirming gift so be ready to tell your legacy stories. Your promotional literature (see below) is an obvious place to do this but think of other ways including the church magazine, website and social media.

But do you have a story to tell? Not if we have a ten year old legacy sitting in the church accounts and kept back in anticipation of that rainy day. We need to be able to tell stories of how a legacy has made a difference if we want to encourage people to make gifts in their wills. A legacy policy, as below, can be the starting point for your story telling if you have no legacies to celebrate.

Be intentional

A strategy for encouraging gifts in wills is a long term investment not a quick fix, rather like sowing seed and waiting patiently for a harvest. So take time to prepare the ground well and explore the helpful resources that are freely available. The following are some key steps to take.

- Secure the support and encourage the personal engagement of your church council/trustees. Sure, you need their understanding and their green light but you also need their advocacy and visible support as it is rolled out. Ideally some of your first legacy pledges will come from your leadership team.
- Agree a formal legacy policy to crystallise how you will use any unrestricted legacy gifts left to the church and reflect this in your promotional material. This policy is your legacy 'case for support'; it tells how you will use gifts in a will to make a real difference. If your church gifts a percentage of income to overseas mission then clarify in your legacy policy whether this applies to legacy income

---

[83] Applying behavioural insights to charitable giving, pages 22-23. Cabinet Office and Charities Aid Foundation.
[84] www.radcliffeconsulting.org

and avoid a heated internal debate down the line.[85]

- Appoint a legacy officer who can respond on behalf of the church to enquiries about legacy gifts. Such a person need not be a legal expert but they do need some knowledge and a great deal of courtesy and sensitivity.
- Prepare some simple but attractive promotional literature. A legacy leaflet is a must with stories of what previous legacies have achieved (if you can) and an indication of which areas of ministry can be sustained or developed by a legacy gift. Raise awareness through preaching, posters, magazine articles, personal testimonies and don't forget your website where legacies should sit alongside all other forms of giving to the local church. The key is a patient, drip by drip approach.
- Compile a legacy pack for anyone who shows interest which will include guidance on making or reviewing their will with a solicitor.[86]

Above all, mainstream legacy giving as part of your stewardship ministry. That regular, sensitive, year round stewardship preaching from chapter one should include wills and legacies, not least around All Saints Day and Remembrance Sunday. Christian Legacy research found that where legacy giving is taught, respondents were 2.7 times more likely to have pledged a legacy to a church or Christian charity.[87]

Take advantage of Will Aid each November to encourage people to think about making or updating their will as an act of wise and caring stewardship. Use the resources on the YouTube channel of the Remember a Charity website. The option to request legacy information should be in every stewardship programme and annual review and in Friends group literature. Consider a special legacy service in church, perhaps for those who have left a legacy and to celebrate what has been achieved. Consider also inviting a speaker to particular church groups to talk about the importance of making a will and the opportunities for leaving a legacy.

Finally, two important reminders. First, never, ever forget to write and say thank you when you receive a legacy gift. It sounds obvious but

---

[85] A legacy policy cast in the form of a communication to potential legators can be found at www.parishresources.org.uk/legacies
[86] The hard copy Anglican materials at www.churchlegacy.org.uk are excellent and can be customised or used as a guide to create your own. The online resources at www.christianlegacy.org.uk are a free download.
[87] Church Website Legacy Audit 2012.

it seems that sometimes charities forget.[88] Second, the only *advice* about legacies anyone in the church should ever give is to take advice from a solicitor.

In-memoriam gifts

Before closing a brief word on in-memoriam gifts is appropriate. Churches will be familiar with donations to charity in memory of a loved one, often in lieu of flowers and sometimes with sponsored events.[89]

In-memoriam gifts are a powerful motivation to generosity and churches should note that this is an area of growing significance. It is estimated that in-memoriam gifts are worth around £430 million and that around 38% of adults have given in memory in the past year. Many gifts are one off donations but for some there is a lengthy engagement with a charity and repeated gifts and/or fundraising activity. We should note also some tender evidence that those making in-memoriam gifts are more likely to pledge a legacy and to leave a higher value gift in a will.

Gifts in memory of a loved one, including commemorative items, can play an important part in the resolution of grief. They reflect our desire to mark, remember and celebrate the life of a loved one. One of the ways in which people make sense of bereavement is to turn it into a narrative: to tell the story of their loss. In memory gifts can be a helpful part of this process; 'he would have wanted his death to make a difference to other people – that's why we chose to make gifts to XYZ charity'. Such gifts can express something of that continuing bond with a loved one and help the bereaved discover their new identity as a bereaved person. 'Giving in memory may play a role in helping the bereaved to maintain a bond with the deceased, and regain a sense of meaning - as well as demonstrating the social support that surrounds them'.[90]

Gifts at the time of the funeral are understandably the most common form of in-memoriam giving and such giving is aided by the growth of online giving. Memory Giving is a service developed by funeral directors to facilitate online donations in memory of a loved one on which Gift Aid can be claimed. Much Loved is an attractive tribute website which enables

---

[88] Some brief advice is at www.legacy-link.co.uk/Thanking_the_family.pdf
[89] On this section see Legacy Foresight: In-Memory Briefing July 2014. For an excellent summary of bereavement thinking and tentative suggestions around in memoriam giving see, *Developing relationships with in-memoriam charitable donors: insights from the bereavement literature.* C Routley, J Hudson and A Sargeant in Social Business 2013 Vol 3 pages 143-161.
[90] Routley et al; page 158.

the families and friends to post photographs, stories and tributes and to make charitable donations, over £5 million to some 600 charities in the past ten years.[91] The opportunities offered by tribute websites, of which many are still unaware, to help shape the narrative may form part of a pastoral conversation with bereaved families and can complement pastoral practice.

A second area to consider are in-memoriam fundraising events in memory of a loved one. Such events are responsible for almost half of in-memoriam income and their appeal is powerful. A third area are letters of wishes as people plan for their future including funeral hymns and perhaps requesting donations to favourite charities. A fourth consideration is those conversations at the time of death around donations to favourite charities. Sometimes the church that has nurtured life and faith is inadvertently passed over in favour of another charity simply because we don't think of church like that.

This is, of course, something that requires respect, dignity and the utmost pastoral sensitivity. Careful, thoughtful pastoral conversations around and after death are part of the pastoral care that churches are often privileged to share. In memoriam giving can form a helpful part of those conversations which offer time and space to reflect and decide rather than reactive decisions in the busyness of arranging a funeral while under emotional strain. The critical point is that gifts in memory are driven by those who have lost and wish to honour a loved one and not by the needs of church or charity.

Conclusion

A medium sized church had an active ladies group who were not afraid to tackle tough issues and so invited a solicitor to talk about wills. There was much interest and much activity outside of the meeting. However, legacies were not mentioned at all, and no invitation to consider the ministry of the church to which many of those present gave their gifts Sunday by Sunday.

Legacy giving is a highly significant income stream but churches on the whole are failing to make the most of this opportunity. Making a will is an act of wise and careful stewardship towards those we love while a legacy is an opportunity to leave perhaps the biggest gift we have ever made to our church.

---

[91] www.memorygiving.com; www.muchloved.com See also www.justgiving.com/en/remembering

Resources

www.christianlegacy.org.uk: a helpful website from a group of leading Christian charities with a free legacy guide on request.

www.churchlegacy.org.uk: an attractive, accessible Anglican website aimed at individuals; good stories, a legacy service and guidance on wording for bequests.

www.parishresources.org.uk/legacies: practical legacy guidance for churches; excellent customisable promotional resources and an attractive hard copy pack for legacy enquirers. Anglican in flavour but adaptable.

www.willaid.org.uk: an annual opportunity to make a will with a donation to charity in lieu of the solicitors fee.

www.legacyfundraising.co.uk: Claire Routley holds the world's first PhD in legacy marketing. Her site offers legacy thinking and services to clients.

www.radcliffeconsulting.org: Richard Radcliffe is a leading legacy fundraising consultant and his site contains useful resources to assist thinking.

www.rememberacharity.org.uk: website supported by nearly 150 charities providing practical guidance and dedicated to making legacy giving a social norm.

www.legacyforesight.co.uk: in their words, 'mapping, modelling and predicting the charitable legacy market'. Statistics and helpful interpretation of legacy trends.

Legacy Fundraising from Scratch by Simon George (SPM Fundessentials, 2011).

Legacy giving: where there's a will there's a way. Stewardship Briefing paper (April 2014) at www.stewardship.org.uk

7
DON'T LOOK A GIFT HORSE IN THE MOUTH

'Let us remember' said the preacher as she closed her giving sermon, 'that which we render to God is tax deductible from that which we render unto Caesar!'

Gift Aid enables charitable and other organisations to reclaim the tax paid on eligible donations. In 2012-13 Gift Aid was worth just over £1 billion to the charitable sector in the UK, roughly 2% of all income.[92]

In addition, in 2013 the Government introduced a new Gift Aid Small Donations Scheme (GASDS) which in a manner similar to Gift Aid allows churches and charities to claim, via HMRC, up to £1,250 a year on *loose cash* donations up to £20.

Both Gift Aid and the Small Donations Scheme put serious money on the table and rightly so. This generous government provision recognises and affirms the immense contribution made by churches, charities and other eligible groups in guarding our nation's heritage and contributing to wellbeing and citizenship. Both promoting these welcome provisions and administering them well is a vital stewardship task for the local church. With big money at stake we should not be surprised that there are consequences for mistakes; money wrongly claimed must be repaid along with loss of interest and there can be fines as well.

Managing Gift Aid

The basics of Gift Aid will be familiar.[93] Those who pay UK tax can sign an enduring Gift Aid declaration which allows their church to reclaim the tax they have paid on their gifts. It is also possible for individuals to complete a one off Gift Aid declaration which relates to a specific gift, for example when visiting another church. Gift Aid is reclaimed at the standard rate of tax, currently 20%, which makes a gift of £10 worth £12.50 to the charity. There must be an 'audit trail', that is evidence for each gift, so record keeping of weekly envelopes, standing orders and those one off donations is a priority. The church must submit a claim to HMRC, which

---

[92] National Audit Office report *Gift Aid and reliefs on donations* (Nov 2013). Access at www.nao.org.uk and search for Gift Aid.

[93] As a tax measure Gift Aid can be complex beyond the basics. Basic HMRC guidance is at www.gov.uk/claim-gift-aid. See the accessible Stewardship briefing papers at www.stewardship.org.uk/resources. For a detailed, technical treatment see Graham Elliott's book in the Resources section of this chapter.

from 2013 must normally be done electronically through Charities Online, although a paper based ChR1 form can be used.[94]

Managing the Gift Aid basics is straightforward in the main and is not covered here. Good advice is available and cost effective software can simplify the process. Direct debit based giving schemes as described in chapter 2 take the entire burden off the church while several Anglican dioceses offer centralised Gift Aid schemes which make life easier for the local church.[95] It is worth reminding ourselves that as charities our churches are bound by charity law and that many of our church leaders are charity trustees. Gift Aid is only claimable on eligible income and where expenditure is on demonstrable charitable purpose. One free church leader noted how HMRC had sought to claw back Gift Aid because the church could not prove that the overseas project the church supported was charitable in purpose. So let's look at some common issues.

Not paying enough tax

Tom caught the Gift Aid bug early, signing his declaration in 2001 and giving generously by standing order ever since. Which is great, except that Tom stopped working and paying tax in 2010. Abbie signed her declaration in 2008 but although she is working part time tax threshold changes mean that, like Tom, she is no longer paying tax. Dola pays a little tax on her pension and gives very generously to her church.

Quite rightly the Gift Aid secretary wrote to Tom, Abbie and Dola each year to *thank* them for their gifts. But she never prompted them about their tax status although HMRC require organisations to remind their donors of the need to pay sufficient tax. It is an easy mistake but here's the thing: Tom, Abbie and Dola are *themselves* responsible for repaying to HMRC the tax which the church has claimed. To address this issue see the section below on thank you letters.

Can I claim Gift Aid on this?

Not every charitable transaction is eligible for Gift Aid. It must be a voluntary gift, it must be a monetary transaction and there must be an audit trail. Gift Aid cannot be reclaimed on raffle tickets or tickets for social or fundraising events because there is a benefit to the donor or a person

---

[94] The paper ChR1 claim form is available for those who don't have internet access; it cannot be photocopied and is for up to 15 donors (although this can be extended to 90 with extension forms).

[95] For a step by step guide to managing Gift Aid see www.givingingrace.org/giftaid. For Gift Aid software visit www.datadevelopments.co.uk

connected to the donor as defined by HMRC. Nor can you Gift Aid the value of items a church member donates to a jumble sale because it is not a cash transaction.

But there are grey areas. A building project asks people to 'sponsor a brick' at £5 per brick. These gifts can be Gift Aided; they are a monetary gift. However, if the church promises to list each donor in a book or even inscribe names on the brick it steps into a very grey area of potential benefit and whether the donations are gifts, and advice from HMRC should be sought.

Another example: a local hotel donates a £25 spa treatment to a charity auction and the bidder pays £100. Both clear benefit and clear skin accrue to the donor so surely Gift Aid cannot be claimed? Yes it can. HMRC rules state that on gifts *up* to £100 a benefit to the value of 25% is acceptable. The spa treatment at £25 is 25% of the £100 gift so the whole £100 can be gift aided.

The same hotel also donates a weekend break which normally costs £100. If someone bids £100 there can be no Gift Aid because the benefit to the donor exceeds the 25% rule. But, what if someone bids £400 for the same weekend break? Gift Aid can still not be claimed. Why? Because the rules state that for gifts between £101 and £1,000 the maximum benefit can be only £25. The £100 value of this weekend exceeds this so no Gift Aid. Except that, *if before the auction the donor knew the break was worth just £100* then under the split payments rule she could pay £100 for the break and treat the remaining £300 of her bid as a gift and so the church could claim Gift Aid on the £300. However, be aware that there are also limits to the total benefits a donor can receive in a year.

Basically, for much day to day church life Gift Aid is simple and beneficial. But the more creative and complex your fundraising the more complex the Gift Aid issues can become so for anything out of the ordinary take advice on the rules.[96]

Gifts in kind

Inspired by The Great British Bake Off the church council at St Mary, Berry invites the village to donate their tasty creations which are then sold. Can we claim Gift Aid back on the ingredients? Elsewhere Mr and Mrs Ramesh buy flowers each month for the church. Is this eligible for Gift Aid? The answer in both cases is: yes, but you must be careful so read on.

---

[96] www.gov.uk/gift-aid-what-donations-charities-and-cascs-can-claim-on

There must be two, separate, transactions involved and *both* transactions must have a paper trail and, of course, there must be a valid Gift Aid declaration. First, there must be an *expense* claim for the ingredients or the flowers, submitted with receipts, recorded in the church books. Second there must be an entirely separate *gift* of money to the church by the donor, again recorded in the church books. Now, *at least one of these transactions must be made by cheque*. It cannot be two cash transactions. This two stage process must be observed should a church member who incurs legitimate travel expenses wish to gift the expense claim back to the church.

So, what about John and Eleanor who pay for Sunday school materials and see this as a gift to their church? No Gift Aid can be claimed and, we might add, the church is hiding the true cost of children's ministry by allowing this to happen. The couple should reclaim their costs. If they choose to make an equivalent gift to the church then this is eligible for Gift Aid in the normal way so long as they are two separate transactions.

Sponsored events

Norman and Janette are raising money for the church roof. For reasons best known to himself Norman sits in a bath of baked beans while Janette abseils down the church tower. Happily, we can claim Gift Aid on these and other sponsored events.

But - there usually is one - the church like many charities charged a registration fee of £50 for the abseil. Janette raises £500 in sponsorship but Gift Aid *cannot be claimed on the £50 registration fee nor can it be claimed on their daughter's sponsorship as she is connected with Janette personally*. If Janette pays the registration fee *herself* then the whole £500 is eligible. As before, the more elaborate the event the more important it is to consult HMRC guidance and take advice.

Promoting Gift Aid

Now in fairness churches are pretty good at encouraging Gift Aid among eligible givers but there is still some room for improvement. A recent stewardship programme in a church of 150 adults saw 11 new declarations signed because people had been asked to Gift Aid their giving. But some churches are slow to promote planned giving to new members and communicating the advantages of Gift Aid to those who can. There is still a lack of awareness of Gift Aid among a significant number of donors. However, sensitivity and awareness should always be at a premium.

Some eligible givers are anxious about signing anything to do with tax; some are fearful of anything to do with the State for a range of reasons, while a few oppose in principle the use of tax for charitable purpose. We must respect this and but there are still many who will happily Gift Aid if we ask.

Church magazines, leaflets and posters will raise awareness. Gift Aid should routinely be included in stewardship programmes, annual reviews, gift days, welcome packs and any induction programmes. One off Gift Aid envelopes should be freely available for visitors. Above all, have someone responsible for the personal touch and the personal ask which will recruit regular church members. Never leave the individual giver to find out how to Gift Aid their giving for themselves.

Thank You letters

I mentioned briefly in chapter one that it is good practice to thank *all* planned givers for their gifts, whether they pay tax or not. It is also fairly common for churches to write a 'Gift Aid letter' to their tax efficient givers to inform them of their total gift in the tax year and a request to check that tax paid covers the Gift Aid claim on their gifts, as per HMRC requirements to keep donors informed.

My advice is *not* to conflate the two purposes into a single thank you letter for Gift Aid givers. Let your annual thank you letter to *all* planned givers be a genuine letter of appreciation and don't add 'technical' information about tax. Send an additional Gift Aid letter at the end of the tax year to tax efficient givers, including those who give by charitable giving accounts or via payroll, with a note of thanks of course but primarily dealing with the technical issues of Gift Aid.

Gift Aid Small Donations Scheme

In 2013 the Government introduced the Gift Aid Small Donations Scheme, a Gift Aid style repayment to support the work of churches, charities and CASCS (Community and Amateur Sports Clubs). The title is a little misleading; although linked to Gift Aid the Small Donations Scheme (SDS) is not a tax relief like Gift Aid but a government spending measure.

Basically, the SDS allows churches and charities to claim up to £1,250 a year through the mechanism of their Gift Aid claim to HMRC on eligible cash gifts that are *not* covered by a Gift Aid declaration. This means that churches can claim under the SDS on eligible cash gifts on the offering plate and giving through envelopes where there is no Gift Aid declaration to the maximum value of £20 per donation – which sadly rules out all those £50 notes in the offering! My colleague Dr John Preston estimates that the GASDS is worth around £12 million to the Church of England under current arrangements, more if current restrictions are lifted; around £25 million has been claimed since the scheme started.

When a church receives £5,000 or more in this way it makes the maximum reclaim of £1,250 which is calculated (just like Gift Aid) as 25% of the £5,000, assuming that the standard rate of tax remains at 20%. If a church received only £2,500 then their maximum claim would be £625; that is 25% of £2,500.[97]

There is no free lunch. As you expect the Small Donations Scheme requires administrative work and attention to detail for that additional £1,250. This is a new scheme which requires a little understanding and adjustment of procedures to implement so here are the headlines:

- As the name suggests the scheme is for small donations. Only cash gifts of £20 or less are eligible which means only notes or coins. Cheques, standing orders and text giving are not eligible.
- Churches will need to adjust their offertory record keeping to ensure that non eligible gifts (those £50 notes) are excluded and that there is evidence of the amounts given, banked in the UK and claimed under the Scheme.
- There can be no benefit to the donor beyond a simple acknowledgement, for example a lapel sticker. Thus, for example, the purchase of prayer candles is excluded because of a donor benefit.
- To claim under the SDS the church must have been registered with HMRC for tax purposes for at least two tax years, must make a Gift Aid claim at least every two years and have not incurred a penalty relating to Gift Aid or the Small Donations Scheme in the current or previous tax year.
- Many churches in the UK claim as *charities* under the Scheme as you might expect. However, Roman Catholic and Church of England churches, for different reasons, must claim under the 'community

---

[97] HMRC guidance is at www.gov.uk/claiming-a-top-up-payment-on-small-charitable-donations

buildings' aspect of the SDS and *not* as charities.[98] To *qualify* as a community building the church must host charitable activities (i.e. public worship) at least six times a year and, crucially, where there are *ten or more* persons present.

- For churches claiming under the 'community buildings' element, only offerings made at worship where at least 10 people are present are eligible. This excludes, therefore, a range of gifts: a mid-week service of seven people (because of numbers); wall safe gifts (they could be donated outside of the service which is the charitable activity); a service in a residential home (because it is not a community building).
- Finally, note there is a 'matching requirement'. Gift Aid claims must be at least 10% of the Small Donations Scheme claim for the same period.

The Small Donations Scheme is a bonus for churches but please be realistic. I have heard talk about not bothering with envelopes or standing orders for those who do not pay tax and cannot Gift Aid their giving so as to maximise the Small Donations claim. Many churches will routinely come close to or exceed the £5,000 cash threshold which releases that £1,250 but even where this is not the case the wider gains of a planned giving mechanism will most often outweigh the benefits of a Small Donations claim on loose cash giving.

Conclusion

Generous government provision through Gift Aid and the Small Donations Scheme affirms the vital work of churches and charities and offers significant financial benefits. Ensure good administration, take advice if you are not sure about eligibility for Gift Aid and be intentional in promoting Gift Aid as personally as possible. And finally, don't confuse these sources of income with the discipleship task of growing generous givers. Both Gift Aid and the Gift Aid Small Donations Scheme are derivative of the direct giving of church members and supporters, not a substitute for it.

---

[98] For Anglican churches the issue is whether individual parishes are 'connected', an ongoing discussion at the time of writing. Note the helpful Anglican guidance at www.parishresources.org.uk/giftaid/smalldonations/. For Roman churches the issue is that the Diocese is the charity so individual parishes claim under the buildings element of the Scheme.

Resources

www.gov.uk/claim-gift-aid: HMRC Gift Aid guidance.

www.gov.uk/claiming-a-top-up-payment-on-small-charitable-donations: HMRC GASDS guidance.

The Gift Aid Guide: Rules Relating to Charity Donations by Individuals by Graham Elliott. (SPM Fundessentials, 2013). Technical and detailed treatment of Gift Aid.

www.stewardship.org/resources: Accessible briefing papers from Christian charity Stewardship covering Gift Aid, GASDS and a wide range of accounting, tax and governance issues facing churches.

Give and Let Give: A briefing on Gift Aid and how it can be made even better by Joe Saxton and Sarah Eberhardt (nfpSynergy, October 2014). A useful summary of the history of Gift Aid, issue of concern and ideas for wider uptake

www.parishresources.org.uk/giftaid; also www.parishresources.org.uk/giftaid/smalldonations/. Useful and regularly updated advice drafted specifically for Anglican churches on Gift Aid and GASDS respectively.

8
FLYING THE FLAG:THE IMPORTANCE OF LEADERSHIP

After twenty five years of fascination with the American Civil War I found myself standing at the stone wall at Gettysburg, the so called high water mark of the Confederacy and where the Union held off Pickett's famous, tragic charge on the third day. Many powerful paintings capture the scene, the battle flags of both armies flying. Here's the thing: no army ever took a position when those carrying the flags were at the back.[99]

Each church needs a funding strategy or, to put it in a richer way, a stewardship ministry. This means careful planning and execution and, critically, leaders who will lead from the front. Clergy cannot abdicate responsibility for leadership in stewardship on the grounds that they are pastors and teachers. Lay leaders may deal with day to day money matters but cannot divorce money from ministry, mission and discipleship. Money matters and in the local church it needs committed, visible leadership.

We see this in the bible, in King David's funding strategy for the first temple in Jerusalem (1 Chronicles 28-29). David cashes out his vision with two big gifts, from the treasury and his personal wealth. He now has the integrity to ask the leaders of the clans of Israel to give their gifts and the result is that, 'the people rejoiced at the willing response of their leaders, for they had given freely and wholeheartedly to the Lord' (1 Chronicles 29:9). Again the introduction notes that a financial offering for Jerusalem was part of Paul's apostolic ministry while personal integrity around money is required of church leaders (Ephesians 5:3; Colossians 3:5; Titus 1:7; 1 Timothy 3:3, 6:5).

In closing I want to suggest three pictures to illustrate what good leadership in stewardship might look like.

Architects

'I want you to excel in the grace of giving' says Paul (2 Corinthians 8:7) and leaders in stewardship are architects of that grace. They must design and build good stewardship practice which encourages people to grow into generous giving.

Our stewardship architecture will reflect the culture, needs and

---

[99] For the flag imagery I am indebted to an anonymous Lutheran pastor quoted in *Plain talk About Churches and Money* (D. Hoge, P. McNamara and C. Zech; Alban, 1997; page 12).

context of our local church; there is no single blueprint. The needs of a listed rural church, a purpose built community church, a suburban church with spiralling deficits and a church which is financially comfortable but with no sense of mission are very different. Leaders need to look at the numbers, plan what needs to be done. But they should also be aware of and occasionally challenge the money story of the church, the way money has been thought about, talked about and tackled in the past. We think a little more about this below.

It is helpful to have a small group to lead in this area. Often this is cast as a finance committee, better with budgets than the bible, with deficits than discipleship. Build a more rounded stewardship committee with the necessary financial skills but which also understands money as releasing ministry and an aspect of discipleship. Such a committee will be charged with preparing and communicating a visionary budget, understanding the culture and giving dynamics of the church, overseeing an annual review of giving and regular stewardship campaigns. It will attend to the core stewardship tasks and blend the work of the Gift Aid secretary, treasurer, planned giving officer and others. A stewardship committee will be proactive in evaluating and seizing the opportunities offered by legacy income, Friends groups and digital giving.[100] As well as promoting personal stewardship by church members, a stewardship group or committee will also hold the church accountable for its own corporate stewardship – how it invests its income, spends its money, raises its finances.

The stewardship architecture in the local church really matters. People give for a range of reasons and we will never get everyone thinking clearly and theologically about their giving. So our stewardship architecture tries to capture good stewardship theology and practice and make it simply, 'the way we do things around here'. The architecture of generosity in a church will help shape those cultural expectations which are so crucial to good giving.

By way of illustration, working with a finance committee in Anfield we built part of our stewardship architecture when we created and communicated our first church budget. Budget Sunday each January became part of the rhythm of our church year and an annual focus on giving for old and new members.

---

[100] Many Anglican parishes adopt the good practice of a Parish Giving Officer or 'Stewardship Promoter', the titles vary, who champion stewardship in the church and provide a link to diocesan and national resources. See the guidance at www.parishresources.org.uk/giving and from the diocese of Winchester at www.winchester.anglican.org/resources/stewardship-parish-resources/

Here are a few questions for leaders in stewardship to reflect upon:

- Do I feel equipped and willing to engage with church finances or do I prefer to distance myself from money matters?
- Am I confident in my role as a leader in stewardship or am I fearful of causing offence and prefer others to lead?
- Do we have a 'guiding coalition', a small stewardship team with a 'financial stewardship' agenda and accessing appropriate training and resources?
- Am I personally a member of our planned giving scheme and modelling the generosity we seek from our congregation?

Story tellers

Genesis chapter 18 pictures the elderly Abraham and Sarah in their tent, still without the promised baby. Three strangers arrive, are offered hospitality and renew the promise of a child. For the elderly couple the hurt and the waiting make it hard to hear the promise again.

It is a powerful picture. At the door of the tent there is a story of blessing, promise and fruitfulness. Inside the tent there is a story of barrenness, disappointment and doubt. Which story does your church tell?

Too often too many churches tell a barren story in which money is short and everyone is giving all they can. Blame can be laid at the feet of denominational bodies that don't understand, communities that don't support their church or the costs of the pastor and her pension.

The story can be generational; today's congregation telling a story that sounds and feels like the story told by the congregation years before. This story may be articulated by one or two people or it can be subliminal, silently shaping and sometimes shackling the present needs and future ministry of the church.

Leaders in stewardship must with faith and confidence tell a different story of God's abundance and promise and our Christian responsibility which challenges the barren story. This is no easy task. More than one minister has seen ministry stymied by a barren story and inadequate resources. More than one minister, having no stewardship story of their own, has begun to retell the barren story while losing the prophetic voice which should complement pastoral understanding.

This is why preaching, one of the four key tasks in *Giving for Life*, is so important. The sermon, as Craig Satterlee reminds us, is not about the budget but about God's abundance and promise and invites us to reflect God's gracious giving in Christ.[101] Good stewardship preaching opens up to the church a new grammar, a new vocabulary around gratitude, contentment, gift and generosity. It speaks of giving but also of our borrowing and budgeting, saving and spending, the planning and preparation of our financial future. So, again, some questions to consider:

- Have we actively listened to the highs and lows of the shared money story of our church?
- Does our church preach regularly around money and, if I preach, am I confident in encouraging us to, 'excel in the grace of giving'?
- Do our council, committee members and key financial office holders see themselves as 'stewardship champions' who tell a story of God's abundance?
- Do we underwrite a rich stewardship story by thanking our congregations annually and communicate what giving has achieved, the ministry their money has made possible?

Fellow travellers

Finally, no one gets money right and leaders in stewardship are always fellow travellers with the rest of the congregation. Leaders must be sensitive to issues around personal debt and money anxiety. They must practice in their own lives the generosity and financial capability they encourage in others. In my experience for preachers the holy trinity of humility, honesty and humour are invaluable.

The following questions are personal but they are some of the building blocks of confident leadership around money:

- Am I pretty much in control of my personal finances, managing a household budget and careful around what I borrow?
- Am I giving generously to my local church and to Christian and other charities in this country and abroad?
- Do I seek to understand what the bible says about money, personal discipleship and social justice – and recognise my blind spots as I read?
- Do I know my own 'money story': how since childhood I have learned to think, feel and act around money?

---

[101] 'When stewardship is grounded in and flows from a clear and bold proclamation of the gospel and does not replace it, and when God is the subject of the sermon, giving is a response to God's grace, because the sermon provides a word from God, or an experience of God, that people can respond to.' Craig Satterlee in *Preaching and Stewardship.* (2011; Kindle Locations 639-641).

Conclusion

Driving down the M6 early one Sunday morning and inexplicably listening to Farming Today, in mild astonishment I learned that modern tractors navigate by GPS technology which ensures that they cross the fields in the same tracks every time. The reason was compelling: yields up to 20% higher. Without it over time up to 90% of the ground could be compacted and less fruitful.

This book has been about nurturing income streams and developing a robust funding strategy, a stewardship ministry. We must build that stewardship architecture, navigate the stewardship tasks year on year, make money part of the rhythm of church life. Otherwise we have little choice but to keep asking people to give, often from a place of scarcity and as a response to crisis. To do this time and again is to compact the ground of generosity in our congregations and our communities.

The task of stewardship leaders in the local church, by contrast, is to tell the story of God's generosity, to till the ground by good practice and to grow and nurture a generous community whose giving is enriched by the several income streams we have explored. The goal is to resource the ministry and mission of our churches, not just adequately but abundantly, for both our congregations and for the communities we are privileged to be a part of and to serve.

APPENDIX:
REDUCING CHURCH EXPENDITURE

Controlling expenditure is also a stewardship task. Below is a collection of top tips from church procurement specialists Robert Kissick and Russell Stables to help save your church money for your key spends.

Extensive savings are to be had via three procurement service websites:

www.parishbuying.org.uk (PB: Church of England & Church in Wales)
www.2buy2.com (2buy2: churches and charities)
www.churchmarketplace.org.uk (CMP: Roman Catholic churches)

Insurance

Long term agreement - if you are with Ecclesiastical Insurance (the majority of churches are), make sure you are on a 'long term agreement' as this can bring you a 25% discount by signing up to them for 5 years.

Look at your excess – if you have a very low excess (£100 or less) ask what it would do to your premium if you made it higher (i.e. £150, £250, £500). Do you need 100% cover? Would you rebuild if your building was severely damaged, and if so, what kind of cost would you look at? More often than not, it will cost less than the full 100% to clear the site and rebuild. Make sure your level of cover is appropriate.

Check your payment method is the most efficient. A 12 month option without additional interest is usually the best option for churches – ask your supplier.

Gas and electricity

Check you are paying the right VAT and not paying Climate Change Levy - as charities, churches should be paying 5% VAT and yet many churches still find they are on 20%. It is fairly straightforward to change and you can back date claims for up to 6 years.

Read your meter - many bills are calculated on estimates and historical data can lead to very inaccurate readings, particularly if you haven't changed your supplier for a long time. Make sure you provide regular meter reads to your supplier.

Contact the procurement services above for their energy deals – each one has specific energy contracts designed for their members. For example, the Parish Buying Energy Basket pools the buying power of churches, cathedrals, schools, and diocesan offices in order to purchase energy direct from the wholesale market – reducing the cost. 2buy2 offers fixed term competitive energy contracts, with a specific offer for Methodist churches. Church Marketplace have an agreement with an energy broker to source competitive contracts for their customers. Be sure to get in touch with them to find out how they can help you.

If you decide to arrange your own supply always get an alternative quote – renewal rates are often higher in price than you need to pay. Ask different suppliers for quotes based on 1 or 2 year contracts.

Avoid rollover rates – always ensure you serve notice during your termination window to avoid expensive rollover rates. Even if you decide to remain with your existing supplier you should serve termination and negotiate a new contract.

Manage your consumption – consider installing a smart meter, ask your supplier about this as it may be available at no charge. A simple way to manage your consumption is to make sure your heating isn't on when the building is empty – you'd be surprised at how many churches have been stung by no one knowing that the heating has been left on all month, making for a very costly bill!

Green Energy

Consider renewable energy as an outworking of stewardship – look for green energy contracts that don't cost the earth! Parish Buying and 2buy2 both have a group buying initiative to make going green less costly. They pool the buying power of organisations that sign up to help reduce the cost of renewable electricity. When looking at green energy contracts, make sure the electricity is from 100% renewable sources.

Oil

All three procurement services have a discount on oil available. Daily prices are available on their websites and the service offers priority delivery in times of oil shortages. You should take advantage of buying early in preparation for winter – prices usually increase as demand increases, so get your order in early to make sure you don't pay over the odds!

Office Products

The price for paper and other supplies can be high from regular retail stores, online suppliers are often much more competitive and have a wider range of items. Each service has a national office products contract in place, allowing members to access heavily discounted pricing, with free next day delivery, and a wide range of items.

Photocopying Services

Understand your requirements before you speak to suppliers - it helps you ensure you get what you need, not what the supplier wants you to have. Added features can add significantly to cost so strip away the unnecessary bits to cut costs.

Understand how much you print - do you print a lot of colour? Most parishes will print over 90% of their print in mono but colour makes up 50% of the cost. If you print in colour would you be better off with a mono printer and outsourcing your colour print locally?

Change your printing habits – try to reduce the amount of colour you print. Change to duplex printing, print in A3 and cut it in half, always use power save, think about access control and make sure your default settings are always on mono.

Check the small print! Read the photocopier contract before you sign it, as often there can be clauses that can add significant cost over time. If you're not sure what something means, contact 2buy2, Parish Buying or Church Marketplace and they will help you – even if the contract isn't with them! Their photocopying supplier has been rigorously vetted to ensure there are no surprises in the contracts, no price hikes, and that the devices are good quality offered at competitive prices. All the hard work has been done for you!

Health and Safety

Check your requirements – do you meet the legal requirements for your building? Think about what you need and the cost – consider fire extinguishers that last for ten years without needing a service and balance the total cost of ownership over conventional fire extinguishers. These are available through the national deals in place by CMP, 2buy2, and PB.

IT Software

Make sure you are paying charity licence pricing – charities (that includes churches!) can purchase IT Software packages, such as Microsoft Office, for a fraction of the retail price. CMP, 2buy2, and PB all have an agreement with an IT Software company that provides software at charity rates – an easy online solution.

IT Hardware

Understand your IT requirements and check that the hardware you purchase meets these. Talk to the representative if necessary - you don't want to pay over the odds for something that doesn't meet your needs, or indeed, does more than you need. PB, 2buy2, and CMP offer a comprehensive IT hardware contract including laptops, desktops, tablets, servers and more from the world's most reputable brands. The service also includes excellent customer care and after sales support.

Telecoms

Check your requirements – get a free bill analysis. 2buy2, CMP, and PB each offer a free bill analysis for your telecoms, whether it's a phone line, broadband, or a system, they'll analyse your current costs and show you where you could be saving. A wide range of products are available as well as very competitive tariffs from the UK's leading providers.

Buy as stewards

Ensure you get maximum value for the money your church is spending - where you aren't able to use an existing national deal, you can simply ask for a discount off the first price provided. Alternatively try and get more for your money by asking for add-ons to be included e.g. if you are buying a laptop ask for a mouse and mouse mat to be thrown in.

ABOUT THE AUTHOR

Steve Pierce is Director of Learning and Stewardship in the Diocese of Liverpool. Ordained in 1985 he has served in parishes and as Stewardship Officer. He is co-author of the stewardship website www.givingingrace.org and also *Your Money and Your Life* (SPCK, 2010).

Also published by Social Partnership Marketing

Invisible Grantmakers - an annual listing of unpublished grantmaking trusts.

See www.socialpartnershipmarketing.co.uk *for further details.*